William James

LLOYD MORRIS

William James

THE MESSAGE OF A MODERN MIND

GREENWOOD PRESS, PUBLISHERS
NEW YORK

8-85

To

Irita Van Doren

In longstanding admiration and
affection.

NOTE

The Thought and Character of William James by Ralph Barton Perry (Boston: Little, Brown and Company, 1935, 2 vols.) is the standard work on its subject. It is likewise the noblest modern biography of a philosopher. I acknowledge my debt to this great book, indispensable to any writer on William James. Readers who wish more information about James's personal life and professional career should consult it.

A list of the other books I have used will be found in the Bibliography.

L. M.

CONTENTS

William James

"Let me repeat once more that a man's vision is the great fact about him. Who cares for Carlyle's reasons, or Schopenhauer's, or Spencer's? A philosophy is the expression of a man's intimate character, and all definitions of the universe are but the deliberately adopted reactions of human characters upon it. . . . If we take the whole history of philosophy, the systems reduce themselves to a few main types which, under all the technical verbiage in which the ingenious intellect of man envelops them, are just so many visions, modes of feeling the whole push, and seeing the whole drift of life, forced on one by one's total character and experience, and on the whole *preferred*—there is no other truthful word—as one's best working attitude."

William James,
in *A Pluralistic Universe.*

CHAPTER ONE

SOCRATES IN CAMBRIDGE

IN THE last years of the nineteenth century, students at Harvard heard William James lecture on philosophy. Nearing his sixtieth year, he was short, spare, bearded, blue-eyed, vigorous. Bronzed and ruddy, often clad in rough brown tweeds, he did not look like a scholar, or speak like a college professor. He had a way of suddenly pausing to raise a window; he would stand, for a moment, silently gazing, as if he felt confined, as if the open world outside was his mind's natural habitat. His sister Alice thought that he expressed himself and his environment to perfection when he told her that his summer home in the New Hampshire hills had fourteen doors, all opening outward. The doors of his spirit opened outward, too; and there were many more than fourteen.

When teaching, James had an air of shyness, of diffidence, that fell away as soon as he left the classroom. He felt like a humbug as a professor: in that role he was expected to be learned and distribute information, but the only function he cared about was communicating truth as he saw it. His private bogey was desiccation, the occupational malady of academic minds. Genius, he asserted, is little more than the faculty of perceiving in an unhabitual way. In James himself this faculty was impressive. There were days when he felt "particularly larky," when an old spirit of mischief revived in him and he was just like a blob of mercury, so that nobody could "put a mental finger on him." On

1

such days he deliberately tried to shock his sedate colleagues and his students. He seldom failed, and he always enjoyed his success. Serious-minded folk sometimes doubted the profundity of a scholar who was so very natural, whose books were as vivid, as unconventional as his talk. James was amusedly aware that his free and easy and personal way of writing, as he described it, made him an object of loathing to many respectable academic minds. But his liking for academic minds was less than lukewarm, and he had scant respect for mere respectability. When lecturing one summer at Chautauqua, he found himself perversely wishing for something to break the unlovely level of ten thousand good people; the flash of a pistol, a dagger, a devilish eye, a crime, murder, rape or elopement—anything would do.

James liked to regard the world as unfenced, unfinished and in large measure unpredictable. In such a world, he claimed, all generalizations are only provisional; there can be no final truth until the last man has had his experience and said his say. This seemed an odd doctrine for a philosopher who had submitted himself to the disciplines of so many sciences. He had thoroughly mastered chemistry, biology, physiology and medicine. He had won world-wide fame as a psychologist; indeed, he was accounted one of the founders of modern psychology. Nevertheless, he asserted that the imposing laws of science, so impressive to laymen, are only approximations, that no theory is absolutely a transcript of reality, eternally correct. Any intolerance of new ideas, of new theories, on the part of scientists therefore aroused his indignation. It persuaded him that orthodox science had become a symbol of arrogance and vulgar success; that it was all too ready to abuse its power by disparaging and crushing innovations that might threaten its prestige. He felt obliged, then, to attack the smug authority of " 'Science,' in the form of abstraction, priggishness and sawdust, lording it over all." Such attack expressed his passionate attachment to tolerance, without which scientific method was impossible. But it also vented his profound antipathy to pedantry, system, convention, the dogmatic assertion of immutable principles—to all categorical refusals to give novelty a respectful hearing. Philosophy, he insisted, like life itself, must keep the doors and windows open.

Personally, James acknowledged, he wished always to live in the light of the world's concrete fullness. He was constantly sensitive to the gaping contrast between the richness of life and the poverty of all possible formulas. The perception of this contrast influenced both his thinking and his way of writing. It likewise justified—at least to him—those temperamental aversions which frequently spurred him into controversies and crusades. His distaste for systematic logic, formal dialectic and deductive analysis was so intense that some of his professional colleagues charged him with "a pathological repugnance to the processes of exact thought." To James, much philosophical literature seemed merely hollow, fatally lacking in connection with human nature— the product of thinking in terms of shop traditions only. In a mood of humorous exasperation, he condemned technical writing on philosophical subjects as a crime against the human race. "Technicality seems to me to spell 'failure' in philosophy," he protested, seriously. Technique was a means for arriving at results, but it was results alone that counted. What was the point of communicating them in a jargon which nobody but other professionals understood? Philosophers, James believed, had a social responsibility. It was their duty to address the largest possible audience, to reach and touch and move the common mind. The world of their discourse was identical with the everyday world of common experience, and he was convinced that there did not exist behind it any other form of reality or being or truth. It was to a world immediately accessible and familiar that philosophers must direct their inquiries, and to this world their discoveries must be submitted for verification. A man's relation to this world, as a philosopher, was not essentially different from his relation to it as a daily participant in the practical current of events. So James, like Emerson, insisted that there is "just man thinking, whether he be greengrocer or metaphysician."

This fundamentally Socratic attitude was reflected in James's way of writing. Many of his books took the initial form of popular lectures, which James treated as if they were a form of intercourse, assuming a common interest, a common understanding, and a friendly meeting of minds. But even the books which did not originate in lectures were conceived in the spirit of dialogue, of direct communion with an individual reader. In expression, he deliberately chose to be suggestive rather than precise. For the exposition of ideas, he used the language of insight and feeling, so that he seemed always to be invoking a vision of possibilities, inviting his readers, as it were, to share the adventure of an exploration with all its hazards; but for a verdict on its outcome, appealing only to their personal experience, their imagination and their native wisdom. The problems of literary method were, to James, a lifelong interest—much of his later correspondence with his brother Henry centered on the discussion of Henry's novels—and his own books, for all their effect of spontaneity, were carefully wrought. He detested obscurity, and considered tediousness and pretentiousness equally unforgivable. So he wished his writing to have the qualities of lightness, clearness, energy and brevity, for these might evoke the "dramatic human relationship" with his readers to which he aspired.

Whether in thought, expression or conduct, James implied that colloquialism was the best rule and vivacity the most fruitful attitude. Sometimes he gave the impression that nonconformity was the only standard he thought it important to conform to. His sister Alice once remarked of him that he seemed "to be born afresh every morning." This, he felt, was the natural condition of science and philosophy; he wanted also to make it the condition of life and society. For reality, he insisted, is not a finished product, but a transitive process, a continuous meaningful change. Life as it concretely came wore the air "of being, or at least of involving, a muddle and a struggle, with an 'ever not quite' to all our formulas, and novelty and possibility forever leaking in."

In youth, James was not reconciled to his own flexibility, his readiness to meet life on its own terms as it came. "Almost any opinion I have now is liable to be changed or even reversed by the experience of tomorrow," he noted ruefully at the age of twenty-five. Forty years later, in 1907, he announced this propensity as a kind of obligation, the first step in a method for dealing efficaciously with experience itself. Characteristically, he recommended the method as absolutely the only philosophy with *no* humbug in it. He put forward his theory under the forbidding label of "pragmatism," but this strange word, he said, was only a new name for some old ways of thinking. However, the book in which he described them pleased him. He thought it a very unconventional utterance, and told Henry James that, after a decade, it might even be rated as epoch-making. Confident as he seemed of its eventual prestige, he was unprepared for its immediate extraordinary success. *Pragmatism* swept across the country; edition after edition was quickly exhausted; it was almost as widely read in Europe as in the United States. Many of its readers must have felt, with Henry James, astonished by the extent to which, all their lives, they had "unconsciously pragmatized." The reception of his book gave William James a unique authority. In him, as only before in Emerson, the American people recognized a philosopher who expressed their interests, their temper, their native way of apprehending life.

As in the case of Emerson, this national recognition did not signify the immediate and total victory of the body of ideas which James put forward. It was, rather, a response to the central spirit of his philosophy. His moral attitude, his outlook, like Emerson's, were felt to be provocative and potent. As thinkers, both men gained ascendancy by virtue of their challenges, not their particular conclusions. The victory of their doctrines followed, and in the same fashion. Their ideas gradually filtered into the mainstream of popular American thought, and almost anonymously became part of the intellectual equipment of later generations. Both Emerson and James proclaimed certain doctrines that seemed to express the inarticulate beliefs of their contemporaries, and these achieved a sudden dazzling prosperity. But both men likewise declared other convictions that ran counter to the spirit of their times; in general, it was these which, long afterward, made their thought seem prospective and prophetic. The resemblance of James to Emerson is most apparent, however, in the object of his quest. This, as a young man, James defined in words which Emerson himself might have written. His hope, James asserted, was to develop a theory of life that would fulfill "the desire of the heart to be a match for the whole universe and not to shrivel to an infinitesimal accident within it." To this statement, he added a characteristic observation: "The way is open to us—we walk it at our risk."

The theory of life which James developed is deeply stamped with his individuality; in it, his character and temperament confront us at every turn. But it has another aspect, equally noteworthy. It is the product of a particular era and environment, which it reflects so faithfully and so fully that it constitutes, today, one of the major expressions of an America in transition. In his personal existence, James had little sustained or intimate contact with the bustling, competitive, inchoate America that surrounded him, the new order that began its rise after the Civil War. Yet the career of his mind was strongly influenced by the dynamism and tensions of this new America. The range of his thinking came to include many of the country's emergent problems—social, political and economic. The very character of his thought was qualified by traits that were being powerfully asserted in the national life and were already shaping the American future. The philosophy of William James incorporated, as vital elements, the nation's experimentalism and expansiveness; its commitment to spectacular risks; its adventurousness and confidence in the future; its belief in plasticity, progress and free invention. Thus, intellectually, James represented his time and place. But his spiritual loyalties, bred by the America of his youth, were fixed on ideals which the America of his maturity gave scant promise of realizing. By insisting that the current state of things is always capable of being transformed, James expressed in philosophy both the actual movement of American life and the genuine conviction of a majority of his countrymen. The line of development which his philosophy envisaged, the kind of transformation that he proposed, have not yet been made effective. The moral vision of William James continues to challenge twentieth-century America.

James grew up in a household which relished ideas and made argument about them its normal form of family intercourse. His father, Henry James the elder, was a son of one of America's earliest millionaires. He was an uncompromising individualist, a philosopher by vocation, a mystic addicted to the darker problems of theology. After a morbid depression which led to a pathological crisis, he became a Swedenborgian, but his incorrigible nonconformity expressed itself in his faith, as in everything else. A utopian socialist, he distrusted all social systems on principle. A truculent democrat, he asserted that a crowded horsecar was the nearest approach to heaven on earth—but he associated chiefly with the intellectual elite of England and the United States. Convinced that life is deeply tragic, he was considered a humorist of the first water. Though his books found few readers and his philosophy won no disciples, he achieved some repute as a thinker.

This unheeded seer gave his children, on principle, a highly irregular education. During William's childhood the family moved restlessly to and from Europe, seldom settling anywhere. William acquired a taste for cosmopolitanism and an idiomatic facility in several languages. His health was never robust, and he became a lifelong victim of neurasthenia. Even as a child in Europe, he showed a strong predilection for science, going in for "experiments," playing with chemicals, galvanic batteries, marine animals in splashy aquaria, and taking curious drugs. In his eighteenth year, he suddenly became obsessed by the project of "giving myself up to art." The family eccentrically migrated from Paris to Newport; as Henry James recalled with amusement, "We went home to learn to paint." William James entered the studio of William Morris Hunt, the friend and disciple of Millet, where John La Farge also was a student. Long afterward, La Farge declared that James had shown promise of becoming a remarkable, perhaps a great painter. James detected no such promise, and his passion for art evaporated as abruptly as it had appeared. But the technical training he received left permanent effects; notably on his way of visualizing the concrete world, and on his highly pictorial literary style.

Persuaded, now, that science was his true vocation, James entered the Lawrence Scientific School at Harvard. The Civil War had meanwhile broken out. Its tremendous moral and political issues fully engaged Henry James the elder, and his two youngest sons presently enlisted. But William James, like his brother Henry, considered himself excluded from active service by physical disability. Although in later years he was to become an active partisan in public affairs, there is no evidence that he was preoccupied by the inescapable issues of the Civil War, and his detachment from the greatest adventure of his generation may have contributed to his breakdown shortly after its conclusion.

At Harvard, James first devoted himself to chemistry, but soon chose biology as his field of study. The Darwinian theory of evolution had precipitated world-wide controversy, and the forces of science and religion were already preparing for a bitter conflict which was to terminate only at the end of the century. It was the implications of this conflict that turned James to the serious study of philosophy, which he began while concentrating on the biological sciences. He entered Harvard Medical School, but interrupted his course to join a scientific expedition to Brazil led by Louis Agassiz. Returning after a year, he resumed his medical course and served a brief internship in a hospital. An attack of neurasthenia followed, and he went to Germany, hoping to continue his studies while regaining his health. He remained there nearly two years, attending university courses in physiology, but he felt incapable of undertaking experimental research; this incapacity was later reflected in his pronounced distaste for laboratory work and his skepticism about the value of its results. Meanwhile, he read intensively in general literature and philosophy, and studied the new technical works on psychology, which was being established as an independent branch of science by German and French investigators.

When he returned to the United States, James completed his medical course and received his degree. He had never intended to practice medicine; he proposed to teach physiology. But any active career suddenly became impossible. His neurasthenia worsened, and he fell into an extreme melancholia. This mental illness, producing a total paralysis of his will, continued for five years. It culminated in a crisis of spiritual despair, and James, like his father, suffered a devastating incidence of hallucination. He, too, mastered his crisis by an act of faith. He came upon the doctrine of free will proposed by the French philosopher Charles Renouvier: "The sustaining of a thought because I choose to when I might have other thoughts." This, for James, was a revolutionary insight, destined to color all his future thinking. "My first act of free will," he resolved, "shall be to believe in free will." Thereafter, he never relinquished his will to believe. In one respect, the effect of James's breakdown and long, painful recovery proved to be decisive. The experience made him a philosopher by necessity as well as inclination. It likewise yielded an intuition which became his most fruitful single concept in psychology, ethics and metaphysics; which served in the end as a foundation for his theory of knowledge as well as his theory of truth. James emerged from his dark night of the soul with a sense that thought is functional; that it has a practical utility; that its goal is action and its value is determined by its consequences.

What James urgently required was a theory of life both scientifically tenable and spiritually propitious. It was a need deeply felt by intelligent young Americans after the Civil War. The impact of the new science, the weakening of old religious faiths, the swift changes overtaking the society in which they were living, conspired to make them take stock of their world and their beliefs. All the members of James's circle in Cambridge responded to this compulsion. All, like James himself, tried to formulate attitudes to life that would solve their common perplexity. Philosophy was not only an addiction but an enterprise, and it solicited the minds of men as unlike in temperament as the lawyer Oliver Wendell Holmes, the historians Henry Adams and John Fiske, the mathematician Chauncey Wright, the logician Charles Sanders Peirce. Some of them saw, in the new science, and in the new industrialism that promised to transform America, evidence that the individual had a free, active, essentially creative role in society; that men could, in effect, bring about radical changes in their environment and institutions. Others drew very different conclusions. In their view, the Darwinian principles of evolution deprived man of his formerly privileged place in nature, while the latest doctrines of the physicists indicated that nature itself was a mechanism. To them, man's freedom appeared to be a gross illusion. His destiny was inexorably determined by mechanical laws, and what he conceitedly acclaimed as progress was merely an automatic, impersonal process, the expression of a blind force or an inevitable fate.

This was the ultimate issue that haunted the minds of James and his friends. Three of them, in the early days of his philosophizing, were intellectual adversaries whose influence had permanent effects. With Oliver Wendell Holmes, for a time his most intimate companion, James spent many evenings "twisting the tail of the cosmos." Though Holmes had chosen the law as his profession, at bottom he hankered for philosophy, and it was as a philosopher that he approached the law and later expounded it. "I always say the chief end of man is to form general propositions—adding that no general proposition is worth a damn." This observation of his old age crystallized a lifelong attitude. What Holmes appropriated from the new science was its technique of doubting, its suggestion that knowledge begins in skepticism. He wished, he said, to multiply his skepticisms, and he soon came to believe that all certainty is an illusion. To him, the finality of force was obvious, and he thought it foolish to exaggerate man's place in the scheme of things. Man, being born to act, was a predestined idealist, since to act is to affirm the worth of an end, and to persist in that affirmation is to frame an ideal. Yet that one ideal was ethically superior to another,

Holmes would not admit. Ethical systems were social improvisations expressed in terms of emotion, affirming values that could be tested only by their immediate expediency. In the unending competition of ideals, Holmes refused to become a partisan; his skepticism was thoroughgoing, his irony pervasive, his moral detachment extreme.

The fundamental premises of Holmes and James were identical, as were many of their major conclusions. But James's skepticism was limited. He had neither taste nor gift for irony. As a psychologist he considered moral partisanship inevitable, and as a philosopher he declared it to be an obligation. Nothing seemed more perverse to him than to make doubt itself one's vital faith. For James, at heart, was profoundly religious. Although for him experience was the only reality, and experiment the only avenue to knowledge and control, he recognized the existence of a realm in which belief was an experimental act, and the only one possible. Within that realm, he surmised, the individual might properly insist "on having something which will answer for his interests in the highest sense."

It was this intuition which brought him into conflict with another friendly antagonist, Chauncey Wright. In later years, James frequently acknowledged his debt to Wright, his "tough-minded old friend" whose best work had been done in conversation, who was the "great mind of a village," who confidently declared that "behind the bare phenomenal facts . . . there is *nothing*." A dozen years older than James, Wright was a mathematical genius. He held that scientific thinking—for him, the only valid kind—must be rigorously experimental and descriptive. The physical order of nature, he affirmed, revealed no spiritual intent; it was just "cosmical weather," ceaselessly doing and undoing. Wright strengthened James's reverence for fact, and encouraged his dedication to scientific method. Yet James felt that there was something uncanny, something repugnant to common sense, about a universe which, like Wright's, was stripped so stark naked as to become only a "nulliverse." Things must have a significance over and above their bare actuality. To Wright, metaphysics was pure nonsense. To James, metaphysics meant an unusually obstinate attempt to think clearly and consistently, to gain the maximum possible insight into the world as a whole. By reducing the world as a whole to an aggregate of independent phenomena, Wright hardened James's determination to prove that it was something more.

It was Charles Sanders Peirce, however, who exercised the most powerful, continuous and important influence on James's philosophy. The two men were, from youth, warm friends and inveterate duellists. "Your mind and mine are as little adapted to understanding one another as two minds could be," Peirce wrote to James when both had passed their sixtieth year; throughout their careers, each habitually complained that the other was obscure, or incomprehensible. What it amounted to was that each attached different meanings to the same ideas. When James publicly announced that Peirce was the true founder of pragmatism, Peirce accepted the attribution but felt obliged to dissociate himself from the philosophy sponsored by James.

The promise of greatness, the quality of genius, were detected in Peirce by all his early associates. He was conceded to be a master of mathematics, physics and logic; he seemed destined to take a commanding position among the philosophers of his generation. Instead, largely because of his thorny personality and the bristling difficulties with which his writing abounded, Peirce suffered from prolonged ˙neglect and sank into embittered obscurity. It was not unusual for him, he said, to pass four or five months in a silence broken only by half a dozen brief chats with his wife; and he acknowledged that the great works which he was capable of writing would never be written. He felt it to be "an indispensable requisite of science that it should have a recognized technical vocabulary, composed of words so unattractive that loose thinkers are not tempted to use them." His own characteristic vocabulary was of that sort, and other thinkers were not even tempted to try to understand it. But for James he proved to be an inexhaustible fountain of suggestion. To Peirce, James was indebted for ideas which he charged with unauthorized implications, for doctrines which he applied in ways repugnant to their author; yet it is the fertility of these appropriated fruits that, on the whole, today rescues Peirce from oblivion.

Was man the master or creature of his environment? Was he a social agent, or only a hapless social product? On this crucial problem, Peirce and James felt alike, but thought very differently. To James, any form of determinism was profoundly unacceptable. Scientific fatalism seemed to him no less deadly than theological predestination. Both imprisoned men in an inevitable, foreknown future, a kind of doom that deprived life of any ethical significance. Trained as a scientist, he had no illusions about the finality of any scientific doctrine. As a psychologist, he understood better than many of his contemporaries the decisive part which desire and will play in all change—even the most momentous social changes. So it was natural that he should found the whole structure of his philosophy on one very simple fact. The fact was that we cannot live at all without some degree of faith.

CHAPTER TWO

"THE KNOWER IS AN ACTOR"

A T the age of forty-eight, James achieved eminence and fame
in the world of science. Such was the immediate effect of
his first book, *The Principles of Psychology*. This massive
work had been nourished by more than twenty years of intensive
study and fifteen years of teaching, and James spent twelve years
writing it. It was a treatise intended for students. But, as John
Dewey pointed out at the time, it exploded the ancient super-
stition that works of science, to be authoritative, had also to be
deadly dull. For James, as his old friend the novelist William
Dean Howells declared, wrote with a poetic sense of his facts, and
with an artistic pleasure in their presentation. The book was,
indeed, as remarkable for its literary art as for its scientific importance.

It portrayed the life of the mind vividly, with subtle insight,
with an incomparable richness of concrete illustration. James,
from childhood, had despised "closet naturalists"; his ambition to
become a "field observer" had been fortified by Louis Agassiz;
and the variety and range of his sources proved to be astonishing.
He rejected no quarter of human experience, however shady or
unorthodox, that yielded pregnant facts. This extreme catholicity
accented the book's suggestiveness, pointed it toward the future.
As James acknowledged, it offered no closed system, but incorporated a mass of descriptive material running out into queries that
were necessarily left unanswered. Meanwhile, he asserted, "the

14

best mark of health that a science can show is this unfinished-seeming front."

Great books are either reservoirs or watersheds. They sum up and transmit the antecedent past, or they initiate the flow of the future. Sixty years after its publication, the *Principles* appears to be one of the major watersheds of twentieth-century thought. Directly or indirectly, its influence had penetrated politics, jurisprudence, sociology, education and the arts. In the domain of psychology, it had foreshadowed nearly all subsequent developments of primary importance. Viewed retrospectively, the permanent significance of the *Principles* was incentive. It explored possibilities and indicated directions. These led, eventually, into social, applied and experimental psychology; into the study of exceptional mental states, subliminal consciousness and psychopathology. Because of its extreme fertility in the materials for hypothesis, most of the competitive schools of psychological theory that arose during the first half of the century could claim common ancestry in the *Principles*, for at some point it implied their basic assumptions.

James proposed in the *Principles* to apply the concept of evolution to the explanation of mind. In this project Herbert Spencer had preceded him. Spencer dealt with the life of the mind as a process of continuous adjustment to its external environment. But he defined adjustment as adaptation, thus assigning a passive role to the mind, and making it merely plastic to its environment. To this James vigorously dissented. He appealed to Darwin's theory of accidental or spontaneous variation, asserting that it was as fruitful for psychology as for biology. Was variation to be attributed to environment alone? James denied it. To give any clear description of the facts of psychology was impossible, he claimed, without restoring to the mind, at every step, an active originality, a spontaneous productivity that Spencer ignored. "The knower is an actor," James contended in an essay on Spencer. "Mental interests, hypotheses, postulates, so far as they are bases for human action—action which to a great extent transforms the world—help to *make* the truth which they declare. In other words, there belongs to mind from its birth upwards a spontaneity, a vote." This was the cardinal assumption of his psychology, and his philosophy also; in one sense, the *Principles* formed the matrix of pragmatism.

The assumption yielded other doctrines. Mind, James insisted, must be conceived as functional, as an instrument enabling the individual not only to adjust to the existing environment but likewise to produce changes in it propitious to his welfare. The thinking and feeling portions of our life, he declared, are significant chiefly as halfway houses towards behavior, or action. Consciousness exists only for the sake of the conduct which it introduces, and its peculiar characteristics can be explained by their practical utility. James conceived all mental operations as being essentially purposeful and therefore selective. Mind expresses itself in actions performed to realize an end—actions which reveal a choice of means. The effect of these doctrines was to emphasize the creative opportunity of the individual.

One of James's major innovations in psychology was his account of the process of thought, which led to his now famous, classic concept of the nature of consciousness. Earlier psychologists had assumed that sensation was the simplest mental fact, from which the mind proceeded synthetically to develop its more complex processes and forms of knowledge. To this James opposed a revolutionary thesis: "No one ever had a simple sensation by itself. Consciousness, from our natal day, is of a teeming multiplicity of objects and relations, and what we call simple sensations are results of discriminative attention, pushed often to a very high degree." The primary mental fact, he argued, is that thinking of some sort goes on. The process involves four important characteristics. Every thought is part of a personal consciousness. Within the individual consciousness thought is constantly changing and sensibly continuous. It always appears to deal with objects independent of itself; and it is interested in some parts of them to the exclusion of others, welcoming or rejecting, constantly exercising choice.

The perpetual fluency of thought deeply impressed James. Our states of mind are never the same, and every thought, even of an identical fact, is strictly unique. The recurrence of the fact automatically imposes a fresh way of thinking; the fact is apprehended in new and different relations. But our thought likewise carries with it the dim context of all previously apprehended relationships. Thus, James argued, "Experience is remoulding us every moment, and our mental reaction on every given thing is really a resultant of our experience of the whole world up to that date." The higher states of consciousness are not compounded from lower states; even the most complex thought conceivable is single and indivisible, transitory and unique. Fluency, continuous change, is the dominant characteristic of mental life. In its essential nature, consciousness resembles a river. Let us, James proposed, call it "the stream of thought, of consciousness, or of subjective life."

The "wonderful stream of our consciousness," James observed, is forever qualified by a change of pace; "like a bird's life, it seems to be made up of an alternation of flights and perchings." The halts, or perchings, he ascribed to the substantive parts of the stream, the immediate perception of fact. The flights, or transitive parts, leading from one conclusion to another, are made up of perceptions of relationship and feelings of tendency. It is these which invest our thinking with richness and significance, which convert acquaintance with a thing into true knowledge about it. In consciousness, James asserted, these perceptions of relationship and feelings of tendency exist as a dim, penumbral context, a kind of psychic overtone, suffusion, or fringe. But, because it is this fringe which makes thinking dynamic, as well as significant and rich, James emphasized its psychological importance. It is, he said, "the free water of consciousness that psychologists resolutely overlook," and he continued to deal with it, in one way or another, to the very end of his life. As a largely uncharted province of "functional psychology," James made "the twilight region that surrounds the clearly lighted center of experience" a permanent and central interest, with results to be noted later.

According to James, the mind is always a theater of simultaneous possibilities. Consciousness is their comparison—the selection of some, the rejection of all others, by attention. Our thinking depends upon the things we have experienced, but it is our habits of attention which largely determine what these shall be. Subjective interest governs attention, and in this sense James described every consciousness as being a "fighter for ends." His doctrines of belief and will dealt with the contest. On the level of practical affairs, we believe, and thus endow with reality, anything which strongly relates to our emotional and active life; whatever excites and stimulates our interest becomes real to us. On the level of ideas and theories, we believe those which account most satisfactorily for our experience and, in addition, appeal most urgently to our esthetic, emotional and active needs.

In James's view, will is a relation between the mind and its concepts. It is attention with effort; the sustaining of a difficult thought; the resolute affirming and adopting of the thought, its implications and consequences. The normal sphere of effort, he held, is to be found wherever non-instinctive motives to behavior are to rule the day. Both knowledge and intelligent action are thus dependent upon strength of will. "There are at all times *some* ideas from which we shy away like frightened horses the moment we get a glimpse of their forbidding profile upon the threshold of our thought," James wrote. The only resistance which our will can possibly experience, he declared, is the resistance which such an idea offers to being attended to at all. To attend to it is the volitional act, and the only inward volitional act which we ever perform. Therefore, James stated, insofar as our morality and religion are deliberate, they, too, depend upon our will.

His doctrine of the will, like his theory of consciousness, came to play a major role in James's philosophy. Its eventual importance was prefigured in the *Principles* by a contrast which he drew between two responses to experience.

When a dreadful object is presented, or when life as a whole turns up its dark abysses to our view, then the worthless ones among us lose their hold on the situation altogether, and either escape from its difficulties by averting their attention, or if they cannot do that, collapse into yielding masses of plaintiveness and fear. . . . But the heroic mind does differently. To it, too, the objects are sinister and dreadful, unwelcome, incompatible with wished-for things. But it can face them if necessary, without for that losing its hold upon the rest of life.

This ability of the "heroic man," James asserted, is the measure of his worth and function in the game of human life. He becomes a master of life by being equipped to control his experience, and his influence upon others may radically affect the outcome of any collective situation. For in both the practical and theoretic spheres, we turn for guidance to those who have a head for risks and a sense for living on the perilous edge. Our courage is likely to be a reflex of another's courage, and our faith to be a faith in someone else's faith. "We draw new life," James asserted, "from the heroic example."

Among James's most original contributions to psychology was his theory of the emotions, which explicitly contradicted the assumption of common sense. The theory became known as the James-Lange theory because the Danish physiologist Carl Georg Lange, independently of James and shortly after him, published similar conclusions. In James's view, the general causes of the emotions are strictly physiological. He therefore contended that bodily changes directly follow perception of the stimulus, and that the subjective feeling of these same changes as they occur constitutes the emotion. He summed up this hypothesis in the statement that "we feel sorry because we cry, angry because we strike, afraid because we tremble," arguing that unless the bodily states immediately followed the perception, the perception itself would be purely cognitive in form and destitute of emotional content. In such circumstances, action would be coldly rational and possibly effective: we might see a bear and think it wise to run; but we should not actually feel afraid. This theory of the emotions, also, had reverberations in some of James's philosophical essays.

When he published the *Principles*, James considered the

condition of psychology, as a science, comparable to that of physics before Galileo, or that of chemistry before Lavoisier, and he regarded his own treatise as exploratory but provisional. His hope was for the eventual discovery of causal laws making possible the prediction and control of mental life. Control of its conditions on a large scale, he asserted, would be an achievement compared with which the control of the rest of physical nature would appear relatively insignificant. Almost from the outset of his studies, James recognized the fruitfulness of a clinical attitude, and this led him, whenever possible, to approach the mind by way of its pathology. In the *Principles,* he drew freely on the work of Jean Martin Charcot, Pierre Janet, Alfred Binet, pioneer investigators of the phenomena of dissociation. James treated extensively such topics as multiple consciousness, subconsciousness, hallucination, the hypnotic trance and various aspects of hysteria. Many contemporary psychologists condemned his excursions into these fields, alleging them to be unscientific. But the disapproval of academic circles merely stimulated his temperamental nonconformity, and increased his obstinate hospitality to all doctrines despised by the genteel. He felt, he said, like a man who must set his back against an opened door if he does not wish to see it closed and locked. He associated himself with the Society for Psychical Research, and undertook a vigorous public championship of the cause of "faith-healers" and "mental healers," insisting that there is no source of deception in the investigation of nature which compares with a fixed belief—common among orthodox scientists—that certain kinds of phenomena are impossible, or irrelevant.

After publishing the *Principles,* James claimed that he had exhausted his interest and fertility as a psychologist. He resolved to become "exclusively a moralist and metaphysician." In spite of this decision, he never abandoned psychology. Instead, his interest in psychopathology became more pronounced, and he continued to study those exceptional mental states, as he termed them, which promised to illuminate vividly the central core of human nature. The thought of "psycho-physical experimentation, and altogether of brass-instrument and algebraic-formula psychology," he confessed, filled him with horror. His preference was for those investigations by which the menagerie and the madhouse, the nursery, the prison and the hospital, had been made to deliver up their material. They showed the world of mind to be infinitely more complex than had previously been suspected; whatever beauties it retained, the beauty of academic neatness was not one of them. He was thus predisposed to welcome the theories of Sigmund Freud and Carl Jung, about whose methods of interpretation he was nevertheless dubious; and he readily adopted the theory of the "subliminal self" advanced by his friend Frederick W. H. Myers. The effect of James's later study of psychopathology was to be registered most significantly in his metaphysics and his philosophy of religion, as will become evident. But his early excursions into that field precipitated a conviction that the "consciousness" described by other psychologists was merely a small segment of the psychic spectrum, a special phase of mentality evolved for adaptation to environment, and he surmised that other phases, could they be tapped and controlled, might yield functional accretions of immense importance.

This conviction inspired him to write a celebrated essay on "The Energies of Men." In it, he argued that men possess amounts of resource which only exceptional individuals push to their extremes of use, and that under appropriate conditions everyone might do so. He suggested that the "twilight region" is, in reality, a storehouse of unsuspected resources; that there exist incremental powers available to every individual, provided he can find the key which will release them. These powers are applicable not only to outer work but inner work—the capacity to achieve a higher qualitative level of life. The appropriate key, he conceded, might in every individual case be a different one. Excitements, ideas and efforts are what carry us over the dam of personal obstructions which forbid us the wider potential range, and restrict us to the habitually narrow actual use. He enumerated a number of disciplines which, in his estimation, had furnished impressive evidence of releasing the incremental energies. Among these, he noted that of yoga, the spiritual exercises of St. Ignatius Loyola, certain experimental ascetic practices which John Dewey had devised for his students. He likewise included—as examples of a wave of religious activity then passing over the American world—New Thought, Christian Science and others. These new faiths, he pointed out, had a common denominator: all of them negated feelings of fear and inferiority; all of them, on the positive side, operated by the suggestion of power. "There are in every one," James contended, "potential forms of activity that actually are shunted out from use." This fact dominated the whole problem of individual and national education, and he urged psychologists to undertake a program of concrete and methodical study directed to its solution.

Did not this imply that, beyond the range of physical existence, across the threshold of "consciousness," there is a dimension of being which at present we have no organ for apprehending? The probable existence of such a dimension is assumed by the essays on faith which James collected in *The Will to Believe*. In them, he spoke both as a psychologist and a philosopher, taking the standpoint that our faculties of belief are primarily functional and are given us to live by. What, then, is their proper use? Discussion of his critique of religious faith and the doctrines to which it led him can be undertaken most profitably in connection with his metaphysics. But *The Will to Believe* is not only a study of the ethics of faith. It is likewise an analysis of the uses of belief in our everyday existence. It rests upon James's theory of consciousness and his theory of the will.

His fundamental proposition is that some measure of unwarranted trust is preliminary to knowledge and indispensable to action. We therefore cannot live at all without faith. Even scientists, James pointed out, are not exempt from this necessity: for them, faith is synonymous with working hypothesis. Every man of science has taken his stand on a sort of dumb conviction that the truth must lie in one direction rather than another, and a sort of preliminary assurance that his individual notion could be made to work; he has borne his best fruit in trying to make it work. This "dumb conviction" and "preliminary assurance," James argued, are the genuine basis of action. Faith, therefore, is belief in something concerning which doubt is still theoretically possible. Since the ultimate test of belief is willingness to act, faith is the readiness to act in a cause, the prosperous issue of which is not certified in advance.

This hazardous venture, James asserted, is the method by which human life is carried on. It constitutes the way in which men act with respect to the innumerable practical decisions of daily life where complete knowledge is lacking and positive guaranty of the outcome is absent. In the average man, he contended, the power to trust, to incur a risk beyond the warrant of actual evidence, is an essential function. Without it, action would merely cease. To act on belief is necessary; if the results of action justify the precursive belief, that belief itself becomes true. In such instances, faith creates its own verification. The truths cannot become true until faith has made them true by the test of experiment.

Scientists describe this process as the method of hypothesis and experimental verification. James, dealing with its application to the daily life of the individual, called it the method of belief based on desire. For, in the absence of complete knowledge, the individual takes his risks in the direction of his desires; he is prompted to try to bring about the results he genuinely wants. James held that the wish is father to the thought, that the thought becomes father to the fact. If the individual achieves his hoped-for result—if his experiment comes out successfully—he not only verifies his belief but produces some change in the existing state of affairs. Therefore, James declared "that the course of destiny may be altered by individuals no wise evolutionist ought to doubt."

It follows that progress and evolution are not automatic processes; that living, in the sense of conduct and action, is not subject to determinism. The individual is not a pawn, but an active participant in the game of life. To James, nothing suggested this more eloquently than the fact that the impulse to take life strivingly is indestructible in the human race. Is it not true, he asked, that in the total game of life we stake our persons all the while? Success, he asserted, depends upon energy of act; energy derives from the will, and depends upon belief that we shall not fail; and this belief, in turn, depends upon the faith that we are right—which faith thus verifies itself. James carefully emphasized the fact that there is no scientific or other method by which men can steer safely between the opposite dangers of believing too little or of believing too much. But, he said, to face such dangers is apparently our duty, and to hit the right channel between them is the measure of our wisdom as men.

He conceived the individual's life, and all social progress, as a form of perpetual experiment. But he did not preach reckless faith. The "will to believe" for which he argued is best defined as courage weighted with responsibility. Contingency signifies that no precaution can absolutely eliminate all hazard of shipwreck. The individual must take everything into account that may tell against his success, and make every possible provision to minimize disaster in the event of his failure. But having done so, he must act. And in this circumstance, James preached the right of the individual to indulge his personal faith at his personal risk. The part of wisdom would always be to believe what is in the line of one's needs, for only by such belief is the need fulfilled. Over a wide area of existence, possibilities and not finished facts are the realities with which we have actively to deal. So James argued, and pointed out that "as the essence of courage is to stake one's life on a possibility, so the essence of faith is to believe that the possibility exists." But his doctrine subordinated faith to action, for the real utility of faith is to make action genuinely dynamic. "These, then, are my last words to you," he told a group of Harvard students. "Be not afraid of life. Believe that life *is* worth living, and your belief will help create the fact."

CHAPTER THREE

THE PRAGMATIC METHOD

"THE ancients," William James said, "did things by doing the business of their own day, not by gaping at their grandfathers' tombs—and the normal man today will do likewise." He distrusted the weight and authority of the past. Were not the vital ideals of living men altars to unknown gods? James so described them and surmised that the best life, at all times, might consist in the breaking of rules which had grown too narrow for the actual case. What, then, he asked, could be more wretched than to borrow traditions and live at second hand? In general, he doubted the utility of past wisdom to the present. It might have become only the dead heart of a living tree, grown stiff with years of veteran service and petrified in men's regard by sheer antiquity.

Like most Americans of his time, James lived under the spell of the future, convinced that it could be made wholly different from the present and far superior to the past. A sense of the inevitability of change pervaded all his thinking, and one of his principal motives, as a philosopher, was to show the extent to which we are capable of directing it. Change is bound to occur, but it can likewise be brought about deliberately, and upon this process James acknowledged only one restriction: "The world resists some lines of attack on our part and opens herself to others, so that we must go on with the grain of her willingness." All programs must therefore be framed in the context of existing possibilities. In pragmatism James offered a method for determining the validity of ideas, theories and ideals.

The pragmatic method, he asserted, is not committed in advance to any special results; nor does it rest upon any particular assumptions. But it interprets thought in terms of operation and control, and it evaluates ideas in terms of their dynamic significance—their consequences for concrete experience and practice. In so doing, it reflects a pronounced attitude or temper. James drew a striking contrast between the typical rationalist and empiricist, characterizing the one as tender-minded and the other as tough-minded. Adoption of the pragmatic method implies a leaning to empiricism, a propensity to tough-mindedness. The pragmatist declares himself in what he renounces and what he seeks: "He turns away from abstraction and insufficiency, from verbal solutions, from bad a priori reasons, from fixed principles, closed systems, and pretended absolutes and origins. He turns towards concreteness and adequacy, towards facts, towards action and towards power." For the pragmatic method, like the scientific method, is based upon experimental test.

James credited its formal introduction into philosophy to Charles Peirce, who in 1878 published an article on "How to Make Our Ideas Clear," which specifically applied it to logic. But James himself gave it a broader and somewhat different application. The pragmatic method, as he defined it, maintains that in order to develop the meaning of an idea, we need only determine what conduct the idea is fitted to produce; this conduct is the idea's sole significance. Every distinction in thought therefore consists in a possible difference in practice—and nothing else. Ideas are genuinely alternative when—and only when—they lead to unlike consequences; when they produce a difference in concrete fact and in conduct resulting from that fact. This definition is strictly in accord with James's prior theory of consciousness. It affirms that ideas are primarily functional. Their function is to put us into a working relationship with our environment, enabling us to deal with it, whether practically or intellectually, from an improved position as respects our knowledge and action. Obviously, then, the value of any idea resides in its efficacy to the purpose or intention which evokes it. The idea must be relevant to a particular situation, and subsequently useful in handling that situation. According to the pragmatic definition, ideas are plans for action, ideals are expressions of purpose, and to have any genuine meaning both must be practicable. For the pragmatic method, practicability is the fundamental criterion of worth.

This new attitude to ideas, as James emphasized, was born of the immense advances made by science during the second half of the nineteenth century. These broke down the older notions of scientific truth, which assumed that, buried in the structure of things, there existed eternal "principles" or archetypes of order to which scientific laws in some sense corresponded. But the rapid multiplication of hypotheses in all branches of science suggested that scientific laws are human devices, not literal transcripts of reality. They are a form of conceptual shorthand; they are operational symbols, each of which may be useful from some point of view; and collectively they are only approximations. Reality, as reported by science, in an aggregate of intellectual inventions.

Pragmatism, therefore, denies the existence of "principles" as independent realities. It asserts that they are merely verbal symbols, incapable of solving any problems finally and forever. The pragmatist, as James put it, asks the cash value of any principle, idea, program, or theory. What is its worth in actual use? What results will it produce when set to work in the stream of experience? In this context, the idea or theory will not appear as a solution, but as a basis for further work, as an indication of the ways in which current realities may be changed. Theories thus become instruments. With them, we move forward; and on occasion we make nature over again by their aid. Their great use is to summarize old facts and lead to new ones.

At least in respect to the knowledge that it contains, James argued, our world genuinely changes and grows. Experience, he pointed out, is a process that continually gives our minds new material to digest. This we handle intellectually, by means of the whole body of beliefs which we already possess, rearranging the previous mass in order to accommodate the new material, or rejecting the novelty entirely if its assimilation causes too much disturbance. Our minds are profoundly conservative. We prefer to keep our old knowledge unaltered, so far as possible; we prefer always to retain intact our former prejudices and beliefs. So, as James pointed out, we patch and tinker more than we renew. If we absorb the novelty, it produces changes in the antecedent total of our knowledge, but it is likewise modified by that older mass. New truths are thus the result of new experiences and of old beliefs which combine and mutually modify one another.

In his great book, *The Common Law,* Oliver Wendell Holmes, denying the binding force of precedent, remarked that historic continuity with the past is not a duty, it is only a necessity. James reached the same conclusion about the growth of our knowledge, on which the influence of preconception is absolutely controlling. Our habitual thinking-processes, as he emphasized, perpetuate certain very antique modes of thought, the simple concepts which philosophers term the categories of "common sense." From their remote discovery, these have seemed adequate for all common utilitarian purposes. The structure of language incorporates them. They have, so to speak, become part of the structure of our minds. They are universally used, even by the highly instructed. They are so strongly entrenched in our thinking, James asserted, that no experience can upset them. Yet, in the light of modern scientific knowledge, the categories of common sense no longer accurately describe reality. They are merely inexpugnable anachronisms which continue to serve our routine discourse and ordinary transactions. New scientific concepts have superseded but have not displaced them. These scientific concepts have proved themselves to be more fertile; they have greatly increased our stock of practical utilities, and greatly extended our control over nature. But that they, also, tend to harden into preconceptions James illustrated by the example of the discovery of radium. This appeared to contradict the principle of the conservation of energy, and scientists were profoundly disturbed until Sir William Ramsay found a method of reconciling the novel phenomenon and the old principle.

The tendency in the growth of knowledge is resistance to novelty, and preservation of what may turn out to be obsolete. Thus, there co-exist, at any given moment, several types of thinking which yield concepts that may be mutually contradictory. This situation, James contended, explicitly corroborates one of the central doctrines of pragmatism. The concepts of science are more fertile, but in themselves no more "real" than those of common sense, which they contradict. Both sets of concepts are merely ways of thinking and talking, to be compared not in terms of their absolute truth, but in terms of their relative usefulness. Our different types of thinking serve different purposes in different spheres of our lives. None of them can support a claim of absolute or final veracity. On whatever level, concepts and theories are only instrumental, and the sole test of their validity is the degree to which they "work" successfully. An idea or theory works successfully when it mediates expediently between old beliefs and new experience, preserving the former with a minimum of modification, stretching them just sufficiently to permit assimilation of the novelty, but conceiving the novelty itself in ways as familiar as the case leaves possible.

James once defined his central insight as "the belief that something is doing in the universe, and that novelty is real." For him, novelty manifested the general unexpectedness of things, the spontaneity of that flux of experience which is the ultimate source of human knowledge. Novelty meant change and possibility. It also meant chance which, when looked at from without, may resemble pure caprice, but, when looked at from within the individual's experience, is equivalent to freedom of choice, the opportunity to register a decisive act of will. The only chance we have any motive for supposing to exist, James declared, is the chance that in moral respects the future may be other and better than the past has been. If novelty and change and chance are real, it follows that the universe is still growing, still unfinished, and still plastic. It is, as James said, an "open universe"; and our world will very largely become what we make it.

These conclusions he reached by applying the pragmatic method to a number of the perennial problems of philosophy. Although the method, as James alleged, is committed to no special results, his application of it developed the positive doctrines which make pragmatism a philosophy in its own right, as well as a "way of thinking." To James, the difference between monism and pluralism seemed the most pregnant of all the differences in philosophy; whether we believe in the one or in the many, he asserted, is the distinction that produces the maximum number of consequences. Monism, in the form of transcendental idealism, was the system in vogue among philosophers who had rallied to the defense of religion against the mechanistic and materialistic implications of science. To them, the progress of science during the second half of the nineteenth century signified a world-view which enlarged the material universe but diminished man's importance in it, and which excluded the God of traditional religion. Transcendental idealism was, essentially, a religious philosophy which affirmed that all lives are comprehended in that of a unified, omniscient Absolute, an All-Knower, in whose perfection the evils and discords and problems of mortal existence are finally resolved.

The foremost American proponent of transcendental idealism was Josiah Royce, James's colleague at Harvard, close friend and inveterate adversary in philosophy. Royce deeply felt the moral burden of a complex world from which error and evil seemed inseparable, and he cherished a wistful yearning for final certitude. His philosophy attempted to reconcile a troubled conscience and a devout faith. It made the presence of evil in the temporal order the condition of perfection in the eternal order. Royce's argument for the existence of God rested squarely on the existence of evil, but conceived the ultimate evilness of evil to be an illusion of finite minds, for in the mind of God it would be transfigured into good. The ethical implications of Royce's doctrine were repugnant to James, who years earlier had confronted the problem of evil: "I can't bring myself, as so many men seem able to, to blink the evil out of sight and gloss it over. It's as real as the good, and if it is denied, good must be denied too. It must be accepted and hated, and resisted while there's breath in our bodies." Nevertheless, Royce's dialectical skill was formidable, and for nearly a decade James found himself unable to overthrow his opponent's arguments on theoretical grounds. In the end he was able to do so to his own satisfaction, and announced, with respect to Royce's theory of transcendental idealism, that he had determined to become "actively its enemy and destroyer." As a result, James's application of the pragmatic method to the problem of the one and the many had the dual nature of a polemic and a doctrinal affirmation.

In James's view, monism projected a world in two editions: "an eternal edition, complete from the start, in which there is no growth or novelty; and an inferior, sideshow, temporal edition in which things seem illusorily to be achieving and growing into that perfection which really preexists." James held that the crudity of experience is one of its eternal elements, and that all knowledge terminates, at some point, in mere fact of which only existence can be predicated. The world which experience gives us—the world of vulgar reality, as James described it—has, in the first instance, only the unity of any collection. Our minds endeavor to redeem it from that indiscriminate welter. We postulate more unity than we find, and proceed to discover it. Thus, in the long history of the race, various kinds of union have been conjectured and subsequently verified by experimental test, and others have evolved in consequence of human needs, where action has created them. Yet, when the pragmatic test is applied, the world is seen to be still imperfectly unified, imperfectly rational, and perhaps destined always to remain so. We are left, as James said, with a world in which we find things partly joined and partly disjoined, a pluralistic world achieving unity, not integrally, but piecemeal by the contribution of its several parts; getting that unity by experimental methods, in different places, shapes and degrees, and in general only as a last result. So James announced pragmatism as a pluralistic philosophy. Its essence, he said, is that there is really growth; and it affirms that the world exists only once, in one edition, and then just as it seems. The world of which pragmatism takes account contains "real possibilities, real indeterminations, real beginnings, real ends, real evil, real crises, catastrophes and escapes, a real God and a real moral life," which pragmatism accepts at their face value. In interpreting the world, pragmatism uses "the social analogy: plurality of individuals, with relations partly external, partly intimate, like and unlike, different in origin, in aim, yet keeping house together, interfering, coalescing, compromising, finding new purposes to arise, getting gradually into more stable habits, winning order, weeding out."

According to the pragmatic method, rejection of monism and adoption of pluralism involves practical consequences. As James showed, in detail, it restores to philosophy the temper of science and of practical life, brings ideals into the stream of experience, paves the way for a reconciliation of science and religion. Pragmatism, affirming that order is increasing, is a philosophy of progress. It provides for the genuine efficacy of will, and thus makes the individual a responsible and creative factor in enlarging order, in contributing to the greater rationality of the world. Pragmatism accepts total unity and total rationality as possible evolutionary ultimates, but unconditionally rejects them as origins. It argues for the possible realization of our ideals, for their conditions are partially present; if we live and work for them, our acts will turn them into fact. Our acts, our turning places, where we seem to ourselves to make ourselves and grow, James declared, are the actual turning places and growing places of the world, "the workingshop of being, where we catch fact in the making." Yet, as James candidly acknowledged, the world of pragmatism is always vulnerable and insecure, for some part may go astray, and total shipwreck must forever be reckoned among the possibilities. To adopt it as a philosophy, one has to fall back on a certain ultimate hardihood, a certain willingness to live without assurances or guarantees.

James finally put the case for a world still in process of growth and growing only piecemeal as the author of that world might be supposed to have put it before creation:

> I am going to make a world not certain to be saved, a world the perfection of which shall be conditional merely, the condition that each several agent does its own "level best." I offer you the chance of taking part in such a world. Its safety, you see, is unwarranted. It is a real adventure, with real danger, yet it may win through. It is a social scheme of co-operative work genuinely to be done. Will you join the procession? Will you trust yourself and trust the other agents enough to take the risk?

For in the last analysis, pragmatism could go no further than the presumption that God might require man's aid. Was He not a finite God? And might He not, like life and truth itself, be merely in process of becoming?

CHAPTER FOUR

THE NATURE OF TRUTH

IN proposing a new concept of truth, William James touched
off a controversy that swept across the United States,
spanned the Atlantic and thundered over Europe. Traditionalists in philosophy asserted that truth, like reality, exists
independently of men's opinions; it is immutable, archetypal,
eternal. To the contrary, James affirmed, truth, like reality, is
ever-changing. It is made by men; it grows within the flux of their
finite experience; it responds to their human needs and demands.
Here again, though obliquely, James insisted that distinctions
between thought and deed, between theory and practice, are
futile—because meaningless. Man makes the design for his own
future, and finds fulfillment in living out the design that his experience inspires him to make. The meaning of truth, for the philosopher as for the layman, is to be found only in the stream of daily
life—in that everyday world which James described as multi-
tudinous beyond imagination, tangled, muddy, painful and
perplexed.

The pragmatic theory of truth was developed independently
by James, John Dewey and the British philosopher F. C. S.
Schiller, each of whom gave it a different emphasis. Because he
commanded a wider audience than his two colleagues, James
assumed the responsibility of spokesmanship, and in launching
the new theory he produced spectacular results. It provoked a
sudden roar of battle in universities and learned publications. For

nearly a decade it remained the most hotly contested issue in philosophical debate, and attack or defense ranged speculative thinkers into hostile camps. But the controversy quickly spread beyond academic precincts. In the United States the clamor of dispute rang out in churches, newspapers and popular magazines. By framing the theory in arresting terms, James gained the attention of the general public and excited their interest. Momentarily, they were persuaded that philosophy is a matter of importance to ordinary folk, not merely a trivial, recondite diversion for cloistered minds. For as James presented it, the new theory promised to overturn dramatically many traditional concepts. All its implications were radical, both for the life of the individual and that of the social order.

The pragmatic theory of truth rests upon James's doctrine that ideas are functional, that they are instruments which enable us to deal fruitfully with our environment. Our ideas are parts of our experience, and their use is to help us to get into satisfactory relation with other parts. They summarize and condense, and thus open up conceptual short cuts through the interminable flow of particular phenomena that is forced upon our senses. Any idea that guides us safely and economically from the more familiar and fixed parts of our experience to the less fixed and more novel parts is, for our immediate purposes, efficacious. To this extent, it is profitable for our lives. We therefore believe it, and we hold it to be true unless the vital benefits which it confers clash with other vital benefits yielded by older beliefs with which it is found to be incompatible. The true, James asserted, is the name of whatever proves to be good in the way of belief for definite, assignable reasons. Truth is not an attribute of reality, but of our ideas, our beliefs about reality, and it attaches to ideas only in proportion as these prove useful to the purpose which invokes them.

Initially, then, ideas are true only provisionally. They are true in the sense of being instrumentally true for so much as the immediate purpose envisages. For how much more they are true will depend entirely on their relation to other, previous truths which likewise have to be acknowledged. As James emphasized, for the individual a new idea counts as true to the degree that it satisfies his desire to assimilate the novel in his experience to the beliefs which he has already in stock. The function of the new idea is to mediate between novelty and accumulated knowledge. It makes itself true by the way it works, and subsequently grafts itself onto the aggregate of the individual's previously acquired truths. When his stock of truths grows, therefore, it does so for subjective reasons alone. Observation of the process by which the individual's knowledge—his stock of truths—grows is the first step in the pragmatic theory, and it suggests one very radical conclusion. Purely objective truth—truth uncontaminated by human needs and satisfactions—appears to be a pure illusion. For in the process it is nowhere to be found.

This conclusion, James contended, can be generalized and made applicable to even the most ancient portion of our common heritage of truths. The concepts of common sense, for example, were at one time provisional; they then mediated between still earlier truths and the new experiences which evoked them. The same thing may be said of the earliest formulas of the sciences. But these venerable truths are still plastic, for they are constantly being modified by new discoveries. As an example of this plasticity and modification, James cited the transformation which, at the beginning of the twentieth century, was overtaking logical and mathematical ideas. The old formulae were being reinterpreted as special cases of far more inclusive formulae, or truths, inconceivable by our ancestors. An even more vivid example of this retroactive modification of truth is the transformation which has subsequently occurred in physics. Our whole common heritage of truths, therefore, is constantly being modified and changed. It is in perpetual flux, like the common experience from which it has always derived and continues to derive. And here, too, as in the case of the individual, purely objective and permanent truth cannot be found.

The pragmatic theory of truth thus denies the reality of objective, independent truth. It asserts that truth is plural, provisional and man-made. To conventional minds, and especially to intellectualists, as James was aware, the denial and the assertion are equally repugnant. Unsophisticated, conventional people and intellectualists alike insist that truth is a permanent, inert and static relation. They declare that, independently of whatever we may think or believe, there exists an absolute kind of truth—*the* truth. To this declaration James retorted that the question "What is *the* truth?" is not a real one, because it is irrelative to all conditions. The notion of *the* truth, he asserted, is an abstraction from the real fact of truths in the plural. When examined critically, it reduces to an inaccurate summarizing phrase which serves us usefully in discourse, but which might serve us still more usefully if we remembered precisely what it denotes. The notion of *the* truth is analogous to the notion of *the* English language, or *the* common law. As James pointed out, both language and law are results, not pre-existent principles requiring absolute obedience and unequivocal conformity. Language is a growth; old idiom is displaced by new; usage changes; grammar and syntax, over the years, undergo modifications. Similarly, distinctions between the lawful and unlawful in conduct have grown up incidentally among the interactions of men's experiences in detail; judges make new law by mediating between established precedents and current cases which require a fresh interpretation. At any given moment, *the* language is merely what survives as the sum of all past changes, and *the* law is the body of historically developed precedents. So, likewise, *the* truth is merely our total stock of old particular truths which remain valid. But all three are in the course of change under the impact of experience, bringing new facts. Meanwhile, as James emphasized, "We pretend that the eternal is unrolling, that the one previous justice, grammar or truth are simply fulgurating and not being made."

Application of the pragmatic method to the notion of truth develops additional conclusions. Assuming an idea or a belief to be true, what concrete difference will its truth make in anyone's actual life? What is the cash value, in experience, of the difference between true ideas and false ones? The answer is obvious. In

James's phrase, true ideas are those that we can assimilate, validate, corroborate and verify. False ideas are those that we cannot. We validate, corroborate and verify any idea by acting on it, submitting it to the test of further experience. In doing so, we treat it as prospectively true, as an instrument that will enable us to achieve the particular adaptation to reality which constitutes our immediate purpose. If the idea fully discharges this function, it becomes true; it is made true by the events which occur in the course of our action. The truth of an idea is not, therefore, a pre-existent and stagnant property inherent in it. Its truth happens to it, or befalls it, in actual use. Its verity merely signifies the experimental process by which it has been verified. We know that *that* idea "agrees with reality"; it will lead us, through the acts and the further ideas which it instigates, to the particular experiential terminus which we wish to reach. This capacity for successful leading, which makes ideas true and which is likewise their instrumental function, reveals another characteristic of ideas. They are born of the particulars of our experience, they carry us through a transition which involves action or implies it, and eventually they bring us to new particulars of experience with which, if we wish, we can make practical and profitable connections.

Frequently these connections are not to our purpose, and we are satisfied when we are brought into the immediate vicinity of that reality which our idea has foretold. In those mental emergencies which arise on the level of matters of fact, potential verifiability can substitute for verification. The overwhelming majority of the ideas we live by are of this unverified kind. Truth on this level, as James pungently observed, lives for the most part on a credit system. Our thoughts and beliefs are good currency so long as they are not challenged, and to continue thinking unchallenged is our practical substitute for knowing in the completed sense. The greater part of all our knowing, James asserted, never gets beyond this virtual stage. Is this virtual kind of knowing—so sufficient and economical in the emergencies of our everyday life—likewise adequate on the level of abstract and scientific thought? James contended that it is. Here, again, the capacity of our ideas and theories to lead us successfully to satisfactory conclusions is what determines their truth.

By interrelating abstract ideas, men have built the elaborate systems of mathematics, logic and the "exact" sciences. They are internally consistent, and philosophers have called them, for that reason, "true" independently of any existential reality which they are designed to explain. In this sense, the "truths" that they embody are eternal and unconditional, but their truth in terms of agreement with the growing world of experience is merely provisional. New fact can always require modifications and revisions of these old systems in detail, or substantial additions to them, or cause them to be abandoned for systems of greater adequacy. But until the new fact appears, virtual knowing is sufficient in science; and a fruitful theory may be considered true in advance of complete verification. Since James's death this has been amply demonstrated in physics by the theories of Albert Einstein.

Recognition of the mutability of scientific truths inspired James's most arresting and provocative statement of the pragmatic theory. It was this definition which, more than any other single doctrine of pragmatism, stirred up embittered controversy. " 'The true,' " James declared, "is only the expedient in the way of our thinking, just as 'the right' is only the expedient in the way of our behaving." Expedient? The word was offensive to academic minds, and it outraged all old-fashioned moralists. What had expediency to do with final truth, or with absolute ethical standards? What became of these? They were irrelevant, James admitted calmly. Pragmatism discarded the notions of final truth and ethical standards eternally valid. It proclaimed the truth and rightness of whatever is expedient now—expedient in almost any fashion and, so far as can be determined, in the long run and on the whole. For experience, James argued, has ways of "boiling over" and making us correct our present formulae. "Meanwhile we have to live today by what truth we can get today," he asserted, "and be ready tomorrow to call it falsehood." Since no truth can be considered exempt from possible contradiction by future experience, the "absolutely true" signifies nothing more than an imaginary vanishing point upon which all our temporary truths may ultimately converge. It is the nature of truth to be temporary.

To say that truth is temporary is to affirm that our ideas and theories, the principles we profess to live by, our institutions and laws, and the very structure of our society are all equally liquid. They are effective for only a limited time. They are binding upon us only so long as they "work" in the sense of leading us fruitfully to desired ends. While they continue to work successfully, we treat them *as if* their authority were arbitrary; but we must never believe that it literally is. For practical purposes, all contemporary truths are provisional, but so long as they serve they are not approximate. It is only after they have become obsolete—after further experience has proved them to be inexpedient—that we know them to have been merely approximations.

This distinction is important, and James illustrated it by citing the examples of Ptolemaic astronomy, Euclidean space, Aristotelian logic and scholastic metaphysics, all of which were expedient for centuries because they expressed the current limits of human experience, which thereafter "boiled over" those limits, so that the theories today are only relatively true, or true within historical but obsolete limits. More recently, Newtonian physics has started its journey towards the theories which James enumerated. It retains, today, a relative truth. It is useful instrumentally as a coarse-grained approximation of a more exact system. All these theories were treated as if they were "absolutely" true while they reached the uttermost current limits of human experience. Today, however relatively true, they are "absolutely" false, for we know that the limits of experience which they reached were merely casual and potentially could have been transcended by the theorists of the past, as they are today by contemporary thinkers.

Therefore, pragmatism asserts, our present judgments of truth apply retrospectively to the past, even though no past thinker was led to make them. Thus, for example, the physics of Einstein is now true for the age of Newton; true for us, that is,

so far as we are concerned with the age of Newton. We interpret
the past in the light of our present truths, in the light of a mass
of verifications subsequently made, to which all intervening
temporary truths have contributed, notwithstanding the fact that
to us they have the status only of half-truths. Our present truths
derive not only from our own experience but from the funded
experiences of previous generations; to the future, this massive
stock, bequeathed by us, will become merely half-truths for
further funding. It is precisely because truth is temporary that
truth is forever in process of change, expansion and growth.
Pragmatism holds that beyond the truth of any given time, there
is always a potential better truth to be established later, which
then will have retroactive power. Facts come independently of
our beliefs and determine them, provisionally. The beliefs make
us act, and in the course of our action bring new facts into our
experience; these, once again, redetermine our beliefs. Truths,
James declared, emerge from facts; but they dip forward into
facts again and add to them; these new facts create new truths,
and the process continues indefinitely. The facts are not true;
they merely *are*. Truth is the function of our beliefs, which rise
from them and terminate among them.

Fact and truth perpetually interact, and incessantly determine one another. But since the process takes place within our
experience, not outside it, can we say that there exists a reality
independent of human thinking? This is one of the perennial
problems of philosophy, and James formulated a solution in terms
of the pragmatic theory of truth. Reality is what our ideas have
to take account of. James held that existence is, in the last analysis,
a datum; unexplained and inexplicable, but requiring no explanation because experience conveys it adequately. Consequently,
experienceable reality—the only kind we can know, though
perhaps not the only possible kind—has an element of independence, for in every experience there is something which
eludes our arbitrary control. "There is a push, an urgency, within
our very experience," James asserted, "against which we are on
the whole powerless, and which drives us in the direction that is

the destiny of our belief." The flux of our sensations is forced on us; over their nature, number and order we have no power. Relations, whether mutable and accidental, or intrinsic, reject any effort of ours to deal with them capriciously. The massive aggregate of truths which we inherit—the funded experiences of past generations—resists derangement so long as it can. So, in the formation of any particular new belief, reality acts as something independent; the fact is found, or occurs; it is not made. Yet, in dealing with our sensations, with relations, with previous truths, we enjoy a certain freedom. We rearrange the data to suit our immediate purposes, we interpret the data in different ways, according to our interests. We receive the block of marble, James asserted, but we carve the statue ourselves.

In what we say about reality, our minds therefore exercise a certain arbitrary choice, although the limits of that choice are defined by the obligation to say something useful. All our ideas and scientific theories reflect this freedom; they are human constructs, deliberately designed to serve human needs and satisfy human demands. It is only when our acts bring new facts into our experience that we directly touch a reality independent of our thinking, not yet adapted or assimilated to the humanized mass already there. This reality reduces to a very small and recent fraction of our flux of sensations, or perception of relations, just entering our experience, absolutely unfamiliar and yet to be named or described, or otherwise accounted for. Independent reality is thus "what is absolutely dumb and evanescent," which we may glimpse, but which we never grasp; what we grasp is always some substitute for it that has been prepared by previous human thinking. What we grasp, in other words, is the fact *after* its assimilation; after we humanize it, and reach a true belief about it.

So pragmatism declares that "reality is created temporally, day by day"; that it is created by us. James gave complete assent to the doctrine of F. C. S. Schiller that the world is what we make it; that it is fruitless to define it by what it orginally was, or what it is apart from us. It *is* what is made of it; it is a world that is essentially plastic. "Somewhere," James asserted, "being must immediately breast nonentity. Why may not the advancing front of experience, carrying its immanent satisfactions and dissatisfactions, cut against the black inane as the luminous orb of the moon cuts the cerulean abyss? Why should anywhere the world be absolutely fixed and finished? And if reality genuinely grows, why may it not grow in these very determinations which here and now are made?"

We live by truths that are momentarily expedient and never more than temporary, and we must be prepared to call today's truths falsehoods tomorrow. This fundamental relativity—or insecurity, or commitment to risk—is the price we pay for living in a world still unfinished, in a society essentially plastic and flexible, which we help to form by our thinking and action. The use of most of our thinking, James constantly reiterated, is to help us to change the world. We are free to use our theoretical and practical faculties to get the world into a better shape. We are creative in our mental as well as our active life; we mold our environment; we engender truth, James asserted picturesquely, upon reality. What could be more inspiring than the assurance that the world, the society in which we live, stand really malleable, waiting to receive further touches at our hands?

Pragmatism holds the world to be still in the making, awaiting part of its complexion from the future, still pursuing its adventures. Nothing outside the flux of finite experience can secure its issue. It can hope for salvation only from its own intrinsic promises and potencies. It is a world in which the authority of "the State" and that of an "absolute moral law" are mere expediencies. This world—which to rationalists and traditionalists, as James acknowledged, seems a tramp and vagrant one, adrift in space—is a world of perpetual moral challenge. Such is the ultimate meaning of the pragmatic theory of truth.

CHAPTER FIVE

A WORLD OF PURE EXPERIENCE

THE reality that is independent of our thinking, James characterized as absolutely dumb and evanescent. It is the minimal, unfamiliar portion of the flux which, at any moment, is just entering our experience; in this statement, he used the word "experience" in its colloquial meaning. James also asserted that reality is created temporally, day by day, as the outcome of our actions and thoughts; he meant "reality" in the sense of our everyday world. But these statements, suggestive as they are, describe rather than define; they do not explain the nature of reality. Although James assented to F. C. S. Schiller's doctrine that it is fruitless to define the world in terms of what it is apart from us, the problem of the ultimate nature of reality was for him genuine and vital. Metaphysics had been one of his central interests from the very beginning of his preoccupation with philosophy, for he regarded metaphysics as an attempt to gain the maximum possible insight into the world as a whole.

While James was formulating pragmatism as a method of inquiry and a theory of truth, he was also trying to work out another doctrine to which he gave the name "radical empiricism." Initially, he was content to describe it as a "tolerably definite philosophical attitude." This attitude, he said, was empirical because it regarded its most assured conclusions concerning matters of fact as hypotheses, liable to modification in the course of future experience. It was radical because it treated the doctrine of monism as an hypothesis, subject to verification, and therefore not to be asserted dogmatically. In James's earliest account of it as an attitude, radical empiricism can scarcely be distinguished from pragmatism.

Ultimately, however, James used the name to denote not only an attitude but a particular doctrine; and he applied it, likewise, to "a metaphysical system which has been forming itself within me." Taken as a single doctrine, radical empiricism was related to pragmatism but was independent. One might entirely reject it, James declared, and nevertheless be a pragmatist. It was, in short, a metaphysical doctrine—a theory of the nature of reality—and James proposed to make it the foundation of a system of metaphysics. This system he intended to develop in a purely technical treatise, addressed to professional philosophers and students, but he did not live to carry out the project. Published by his wish after his death, although "fragmentary and unrevised," *Some Problems of Philosophy* represents his unfinished attempt to "round out my system, which is now too much like an arch built only on one side." But if James's metaphysics stands incomplete, the doctrine which was to have provided its fundamental basis is fully expounded in *A Pluralistic Universe, The Meaning of Truth* and the posthumously published *Essays in Radical Empiricism.*

Characteristically, James approached the problem of the nature of reality from the standpoint of psychology. The theory which he developed stems directly from his psychological doctrine of the stream of consciousness, and from his thesis that the deeper features of reality are found only in perceptual experience. Common sense has always distinguished between thoughts and things, has always contrasted them and practically opposed them to one another. Philosophers have interpreted this distinction and contrast in various dualistic antitheses: spirit and matter, soul and body, mind and object, reality and appearance. Monistic philosophers have resolved these dualisms either by reducing mind to matter, or matter to mind. Others, accepting these dualisms as ultimate, have described consciousnes as a primal stuff or quality of being, unlike that of which material objects are composed, but of which our thoughts about them are constituted. Consciousness, in this sense of a mind-stuff unlike matter but equally real, is postulated not only to account for the existence of things, but for the fact that they become known. The novelty of James's theory was that it eliminated a traditional dualism without reducing mind to matter, or matter to mind.

In the *Principles,* James had forthrightly rejected the notion of an aboriginal mind-stuff. He defined consciousnes not as an entity, but as a functional activity of the organism enabling it to adapt to its environment. If consciousness is a collective name for all the mental operations of the organism, are not the so-called "field of consciousness"—the world experienced or the immediate content of perception—and reality one and the same? "My thesis," James declared, "is that if we start with the supposition that there is only one primal stuff or material in the world, a stuff of which everything is composed, and if we call that stuff 'pure experience,' then knowing can easily be explained as a particular sort of relation towards one another into which portions of pure experience may enter. The relation itself is a part of pure experience; one of its terms becomes the subject or bearer of the knowledge, the 'knower,' the other becomes the object known."

This doctrine is essentially monistic. But it is radically unlike the monistic doctrines of either idealism or materialism, which respectively affirm that mind and matter are the ultimate substances of reality. Pure experience is neither mind nor matter, but is the ground of both. In itself it is, as James asserted, neutral. He described it as "the immediate flux of life which furnishes the material to our later reflection with its conceptual categories." He likewise said that "the instant field of the present is always experience in its 'pure' state, plain unqualified actuality, a simple *that,* as yet undifferentiated into thing and thought, and only virtually classifiable as objective fact or as someone's opinion about fact." The "purity" of pure experience, therefore, means its pristine character, its priority to all distinctions and especially to the common-sense distinction between subject and object. Can anyone directly apprehend this formless reality? "Only new-born babes, or men in semi-coma from sleep, drugs, illnesses or blows," James declared, "may be assumed to have an experience pure in the literal sense of a *that* which is not yet any definite *what,* though ready to be all sorts of whats; full of both oneness and of manyness, but in respects that don't appear; changing throughout, yet so confusedly that its phases interpenetrate and no points, either of distinction or of identity, can be caught." This is an assertion that all mystics would dispute, and James himself qualified it in important ways, as will be made evident, when working out the religious implications of his metaphysics.

On James's theory, pure experience is ineffable. Language, being a schematism, cannot report it in its formlessness, and James found difficulty in describing it, even to the point of rendering apparently inconsistent accounts. Thus reduced to speechlessness, we might call someone's attention to some particular field of pure experience by a denotative gesture, as in pointing a finger, but even this tacitly affirms a distinction between subject and object, which distinction is—by definition—not to be found in pure experience. James's philosophical descendants, the semanticists and logical positivists, have subsequently tried to clarify this problem. For James, however, it was sufficient to posit pure experience as something given, a datum, as a ground for perceptions and thoughts, which are real, and for things, which are equally real and made of the same stuff. He agreed with his friend, the British philosopher Shadworth Hodgson, that "realities are only what they are 'known as.' " Pure experience is the metaphysical translation of James's psychological stream of consciousness.

Like the stream of consciousness, James conceived "experience as a whole" to be a temporal process "whereby innumerable particular terms lapse and are superseded by others that follow upon them by transitions which, whether disjunctive or conjunctive in content, are themselves experiences, and must in general be accounted at least as real as the terms which they relate."

It was because James made relations and transitions as much a part of the given as the terms which they connect that he was able to claim that a given undivided portion of experience, taken in one context of associates, plays the part of a knower, while in a different context it plays the part of a thing known; that in one group of associates it figures as a thought and in another group as a thing; that it is subjective and objective both at once. Thus the room in which you are reading this book is, according to James, at the intersection of two processes, which connect it with different groups of associates. One process is that of your personal biography, in which the room is your present field of consciousness—"the last term of a train of sensations, emotions, decisions, movements, classifications, expectations, etc., ending in the present, and the first term of a series of similar 'inner' operations extending into the future." The second process is the history of the building of which the room is part; in this, the identical room figures as "the *terminus ad quem* of a lot of previous operations, carpentering, papering, furnishing, warming, etc., and the *terminus a quo* of a lot of future ones, in which it will be concerned when undergoing the destiny of a physical room." The mental and physical operations here enumerated form, as James remarked, curiously incompatible groups, yet the identical room enters both these disparate systems of association in its wholeness, and attaches to both, equally, in its entirety. In precisely the same way, the room figures in two sets of contexts when you conceive or remember it, when instead of being present in the context of "things," it is remote. However remote it may be— distant in time or in place—it is no less real in one context than in the other. It is still at the intersection of two processes. According to James, therefore, there is a complete parallelism in point of reality between the presently felt and the remotely thought.

But, notwithstanding this parallelism in point of reality, there are major differences between the presently felt and the remotely thought. For James, the moment of sense perception is experience at its richest, fullest and most complete; it also is the

source of our most authentic knowledge. Thought is a substitute
for perception, a second-best process furnishing concepts or ideas
which, to be valid, must verify themselves in perceptual experience, must be convertible into perceptual experience, whether
actually or hypothetically. Concepts or ideas, as James asserted,
"are secondary formations, inadequate and only ministerial"; they
are instrumental or working substitutes which enable us to sup-
plement the narrow range of our perception, and bring our action
to bear on areas of existence that lie beyond it. Thus thought, in
a sense, enables us to transcend the limitations of our intermittent
perceptions, to live fruitfully in the light of perceptions which we
never actually have. It was for this reason that James claimed
that our intellectual life consists almost wholly in the substitution of a conceptual order for the perceptual order in which our
experience originally comes. Yet this substitution carries with it
a penalty.

> Conceptual knowledge is forever inadequate to the fullness
> of the reality to be known. Reality consists of existential
> particulars as well as of essences and universals and class
> names, and of existential particulars we become aware only
> in the perceptual flux. The flux can never be superseded.
> We must carry it with us to the bitter end of our cognitive
> business, keeping it in the midst of the translation even when
> the latter proves illuminating, and falling back on it alone
> when the translation gives out.

The metaphysics of radical empiricism, James pointed out,
proceeds from parts to wholes, treating the parts as fundamental
both in the order of being and in the order of our knowledge.
In human experience, the parts are percepts, which we build out
into wholes by our conceptual additions. Percepts are singulars,
incessantly changing and never returning exactly as they were
previously. This introduces concrete novelty into our experience,
a novelty which cannot be treated conceptually, because concepts are abstracted from experiences already given. Whatever
novelty the future may contain—and the singularity of every

moment makes it novel—eludes the "post-mortem preparations" that are concepts. They are adequate only for retrospective understanding, and when we use them prospectively, we ought to remember that they can do no more than provide an abstract outline or approximate sketch, for the filling out of which we must always return to perception. But the categories of common sense, built into the structure of our thinking and our language, and the laws of science operate to prevent us from postulating real novelty in the world of physical nature. We adopt the theory "that primordial being is inalterable in its attributes as well as its quantity, and that the laws by which we describe its habits are uniform in the strictest mathematical sense." These laws we take to be absolute conceptual foundations, spread beneath the surface of perceptual variety.

Yet, when we come to human lives, our point of view changes, and we see that this is not the case. Psychologically considered, James asserted, our experiences resist conceptual reduction, and our fields of consciousness, taken simply as such, remain just what they appear to be.

Biography is the concrete form in which all that is is immediately given; the perceptual flux is the authentic stuff of each of our biographies, and yields a perfect effervescence of novelty all the time. New men and women, books, accidents, inventions, enterprises, burst unceasingly upon the world. It is vain to resolve these into ancient elements, or to say that they belong to ancient kinds, so long as no one of them in its full individuality ever was here before or ever will come again. Men of science and philosophy, the moment they forget their theoretic abstractions, live in their biographies as much as anyone else, and believe as naïvely that fact even now is making, and that they themselves, by doing "original work," help to determine what the future shall become.

Thus, according to James, reality cannot be confined by "a conceptual ring-fence." It overflows, exceeds, changes; it may

turn into novelties, and can be adequately known only by following its singularities from moment to moment. The conceptual
world is a kind of cut, or excerpt, or selection, from this flux, or
continuum. It is instrumentally useful in representing reality ex-
ternally, statically and schematically. But it fails "to touch even
the outer hem of the real world, the world of causal and dynamic
relations, of activity and history." To gain insight "into all that
moving life," we must turn away from conception and toward
perception. Reality is what is immediately given in experience;
it *is* the experience-continuum. When we are governed by practical or theoretical interests, by the need for action or control, we
arrest the flowing continuum and treat it, in retrospective terms,
conceptually. But if we wish the actual sense of life, if our purpose is insight, direct knowledge of reality, we must immerse ourselves in the temporal flux; the changing, interpenetrating particulars of given existence that form the experience-continuum.

It is in this sense that James's "world of pure experience" is
both an open and a pluralistic world. It stands unfinished; it is
incessantly changing; and even the laws by which we describe its
habits are subject to constant revision. Novelty is one of its permanent elements, and we ourselves help to determine what its
future shall become. From his doctrine of radical empiricism, or
pure experience, James drew a significant generalized conclusion.
He asserted that the parts of experience hold together from next
to next by relations that are themselves parts of experience; and
therefore that the directly apprehended universe needs no trans-
empirical connective support, but possesses in its own right a
concatenated or continuous structure. But this directly apprehended universe is apprehended in its particularity. It comes to
us, at first, as a "quasi-chaos" of experiences. It is not only known
pluralistically, but it exists pluralistically. In a striking analogy,
James likened it to "one of those dried human heads with which
the Dyaks of Borneo deck their lodges. The skull forms a solid
nucleus; but innumerable feathers, leaves, strings, beads and
loose appendices of every description float and dangle from it,
and, save that they terminate in it, seem to have nothing to do

with one another." We frame our notion of the totality on our knowledge of the particulars; but the relations by which that totality holds together, James asserted, are adventitious and not essential ones. The parts thus compose a fluid and flexible world, where unity appears to be in the making as time goes on, and greater integration and order are to be achieved in the future. "The universe," James asserted, "continually grows in quantity by new experiences that graft themselves upon the older mass; but these very new experiences often help the mass to a more consolidated form."

Experience as a whole, then, is self-containing and leans on nothing. It grows, in James's phrase, by its edges, one moment of it proliferating into the next by transitions which, whether conjunctive or disjunctive, continue the experiential tissue. "Life is in the transitions as much as in the terms connected; often, indeed, it seems to be there more emphatically, as if our spurts and sallies forward were the real firing-line of the battle, were like the thin line of flame advancing across the dry autumnal field which the farmer proceeds to burn." In this line, James declared, we live prospectively as well as retrospectively. The line itself is part of the past, for it comes as the past's continuation; and it is part of the future, because the future, when it comes, will have continued it. At every moment, therefore, we can continue to believe in an existing *beyond*. This beyond, James held, can exist simultaneously—since it can be experienced to have so existed—with the experience that postulates it by looking forward to it, or by turning in the direction of which it is the goal. This interpenetration of temporally adjacent portions of reality, of living experience, thus stretches beyond the horizon of consciousness into the future, into a realm of potentiality. In James's metaphysics, experience, or existence, or reality appear not to be confined to actual human perception, but to extend beyond its range. What, then, is the nature of the humanly unperceived? James furnished no explicit answer to this question, although he rejected the Absolute, or universal mind, whose experience contains all existence and all experiences. But the answer is indicated by his philosophy of religion. "If there be a God," he wrote, "he is no absolute all-experiencer, but simply the experiencer of widest actual conscious span."

The effect of James's metaphysics upon subsequent thinking has had an ironical aspect. Its religious implications have had a far-reaching influence both upon Protestant theology and popular philosophy in the United States. By professional philosophers, however, James's religious doctrines, like his preoccupation with metaphysics, have been largely ignored or treated only incidentally. On the other hand, his doctrine of radical empiricism has profoundly affected them. Thus, for example, Alfred North Whitehead, in *Science and the Modern World,* cited James as inaugurating a whole new era in thought by resolving the problems raised by Cartesian dualism. James's postulate that "the only things debatable among philosophers shall be things definable in terms drawn from experience" has become a tenet with nearly all contemporary philosophers who—unlike James himself—disparage the legitimacy of metaphysics. As his former pupil and colleague George Santayana remarked, had James lived to see the developments to which his radical empiricism gave rise, he might "have marvelled that such logical mechanisms should have been hatched out of that egg." But, forty years after he formulated his theory, one of its elements seemed exceptionally alive. James's primordial stuff, pure experience, is in effect a system of relationships. Many contemporary scientists who have been concerned with the philosophy of science, while disliking James's notion of an open universe, appear to agree with his conception of substance. Insofar as they postulate a primordial stuff, it is neither mind nor matter. It is akin to James's pure experience, in being a system of relationships, the ultimate description of which would ideally be expressed in mathematical terms.

CHAPTER SIX

RELIGION AND THE SPIRITUAL LIFE

"I T IS a curious thing, this matter of God!" James wrote in 1881 to the philosopher Thomas Davidson. "I can sympathize perfectly with the most rabid hater of him and the idea of him, when I think of the use that has been made of him in history and philosophy as a *starting-point,* or premise for grounding deductions. But as an ideal to attain and make probable, I find myself less and less able to do without him."

As James candidly acknowledged, this could scarcely be termed a speculative position; it was merely a practical and emotional faith. It was dictated, he explained, by his inability to accept the notion that the universe is destitute of purpose. The existence of purpose required a mind to conceive it, but not necessarily a "one and only mind." "In saying 'God exists,' " he declared, "all I imply is that my purposes are cared for by a mind so powerful as on the whole to control the drift of the universe." The God whose existence James was then willing to postulate resembled man in at least one respect. Both, he asserted, have purposes for which they care, and each can hear the other's call. But in every being that is real, there is something external to, and sacred from, every other. So God's being, James held, is sacred from others, and the meaning of our destiny lies rather in cooperation with His purposes than in the attempt to achieve either speculative conquest of Him or absolute and complete identification with Him.

54

This "practical and emotional faith" was the ground of James's subsequent philosophy of religion. It expressed a personal need of which he had been aware from youth; which he recognized to be profound and insistent; which was one of the dominant motives of his philosophizing. When in *Pragmatism* he asserted that temperament is the most potent of all premises in philosophy, James might have offered his own case as an example. The goal of his philosophic quest had always been a theory of life both scientifically tenable and spiritually propitious, a theory which, in effect, would reconcile the conflict between science and religion that broke out in the middle of the nineteenth century. But this goal was largely determined by James's temperament. A universe that was no more than "cosmical weather," that was barren of spiritual intent, was to him as repugnant as one ruled by theological or scientific determinism. Both kinds of universe stripped men's lives of ethical significance. To this deprivation, James could not assent. Like other Americans of his generation, he felt that the orthodox dogmas of religion had been discredited by science; but, like them, he also felt that religion itself lies deeper than reason in man's nature, and carries equal authority. Acknowledging that it is irrational, individual and often inarticulate, James eventually came to feel that "religion is the very inner citadel of human life." Ultimately, he declared his invincible belief that, although all special manifestations of religion—its creeds and theories—may have been absurd, the life of religion as a whole is mankind's most important function.

In the light of this conviction, it was almost inevitable that James's philosophy of religion should be his most expressive achievement. The books and essays in which he set it forth—*The Varieties of Religious Experience; A Pluralistic Universe; Human Immortality* and passages of the posthumously published *Memories and Studies*—are distinguished by this quality of expressiveness. Perhaps more purely than any other of his writings, they communicate James's vision, his individual way of feeling the whole push and seeing the whole drift of life; that personal insight which James himself accounted "the great fact" about any philosopher. He did not formulate his philosophy of religion until the last decade of his life. But its development spanned his entire career. Thus it may be regarded as the capstone of his philosophy, his final reckoning with issues that he had always held to be ultimate.

One other fact about James's philosophy of religion is equally noteworthy. It is the confluence of all his intellectual adventures, his major preoccupations, his personal experiences. Some of the streams that fed it had their distant sources in his childhood and youth. It was nourished by his biological studies, his knowledge of medicine and neurology, his great exploratory work in psychology, his fascinated attention to exceptional mental states and psychopathology, his excursions into psychical research and the "mind-cure" movement. But it likewise absorbed all the diverse elements of his philosophy: the doctrine of belief, the pragmatic method and theory of truth, radical empiricism and its metaphysics. All that James knew, and all that he was, is represented in his philosophy of religion. It stands as his great synthesis.

His early environment, the recurrent attacks of neurasthenia from which he suffered in youth, and especially the melancholia that afflicted him after his return from Germany—all predisposed William James to take the subject of religion with extreme seriousness. The story of his father's pathological crisis and conversion was a familiar one, and the religious doctrines of Henry James the elder were among the earliest philosophical influences to which William James was exposed. To his father's doctrines James confessed himself always "pretty unresponsive." But after his father's death in 1882 he expressed a wish to "understand a little more of the value and meaning of religion in Father's sense, in the mental life and destiny of man," so that he might "help it to its rights" in the eyes of his friends, who "leave it altogether out." His filial piety was almost certainly intensified by the memory of his own shattering crisis a dozen years earlier.[1] This

[1] His account of it, reported anonymously, appears in *The Varieties of Religious Experience* as the last case history in the chapter on "The Sick Soul."

experience of hallucination and panic fear had left him, for months, incapable of going out into the dark alone, and he felt that he might have grown really insane had he not clung to certain scriptural texts. He was therefore persuaded that the episode had a religious bearing.

The presumptive religious significance of his crisis, which so remarkably paralleled his father's, led James to distinguish between two radically different kinds of faith, and inspired him with an equal sympathy for both. He first drew this contrast in the introduction to his edition of his father's *Literary Remains.* Long afterward he made brilliant use of it in *The Varieties,* for purposes of analysis and description. The "religion of healthy-mindedness" and that of the "sick soul" are not only drastically unlike, but they originate in totally different attitudes to the world and involve metaphysical assumptions that are mutually contradictory. The religion of healthy-mindedness is a fighting faith. It springs from the strength of which we are powerfully aware when in the full and successful exercise of our moral energy. We feel ourselves to be a match for whatever evils confront us. We prefer to think of such evils as endowed with reality and as being absolutely alien, irrational elements of the universe which it is our moral duty to combat and, if possible, to overcome and erase. Thus, the religion of healthy-mindedness is melioristic and moralistic, and it implies a metaphysical pluralism. Essentially, it is a translation into religious terms of the attitude to life which James expounded in *Pragmatism,* with a God who is an ally of our moral wills and who grants us moral holidays.

The religion of the sick soul springs from a condition of morbid melancholy and fear; from human weakness, and the conviction of spiritual failure. It is a religion which responds to the need of deliverance from a sense of the vanity of mortal things, a sense of sin, a fear of the universe. We are all, at least potentially, sick souls, James asserted; the sanest and best of us are of one clay with lunatics and prison inmates; "mere sanity is the most philistine and (at bottom) unessential of a man's attributes." If we recognize this, we crave for a religion which will give us a new sphere of power and a new sense of well-being. A supernatural assurance of salvation will redeem our interior world from waste, wash away our fears, and fill our lives with genuine spiritual meaning. The faith to which a sick soul aspires, and often attains through the experience of conversion or revelation by being "twice-born," is on the whole pantheistic and optimistic. The truth which it asserts is mystical, and is received by the insight of an exceptional mental state. This type of faith implies a metaphysical monism.

James surmounted his personal crisis by an act of faith; he asserted the efficacy of the moral will. From sickness of soul and panic fear, he emerged with the kind of religion which he described as healthy-minded. His first concern was therefore to justify the legitimacy of this type of faith. As a scientist, he wished to defend it against other scientists who dogmatically asserted that science had already made all possible religious hypotheses untenable. This was the motive that inspired the first four essays of *The Will to Believe*, which constitute his preliminary venture toward a philosophy of religion.

He argued for our *right* to adopt a believing attitude in religious matters, even when our logical intellects are not coerced into assent. The theories and doctrines of religion transcend the data of experience and cannot yet be empirically verified. If they appeal to us, it is on purely subjective grounds, and our faith in them is determined by our wills. In what circumstances can we legitimately indulge our will to believe? Assuming that we have carried fact-finding as far as possible, James postulates two situations in which belief based on desire is justified. The first occurs when to suspend decision or to withhold belief signifies losing the possibility of truth, or when to do either commits us to a positive disbelief no more justified by the data of experience than the belief itself. The second situation arises when faith, affirmed in action, will produce its own verification; in such circumstances, "the thought becomes literally father of the fact, as the wish was father to the thought." In both situations, faith is justified by its fruitfulness for life, its consequences in conduct, of which the only applicable criterion is a moral one. "The whole defense of religious faith hinges upon action," James asserted. As a scientist, he considered nothing more certain than "that the world of our present natural knowledge *is* enveloped in a larger world of some sort of whose residual properties we at present can frame no positive idea." To live in the light of that conviction, to act as if the invisible world were real, is the part of wisdom and courage. It may also be the most essential function that our lives in this world have to perform. For our reactions on the world necessarily help to determine its definition, and the very existence of an invisible world may in part depend on our belief in it. "God himself, in short," James declared, "may draw vital strength and increase of very being from our fidelity."

About a decade before making this defense of religious faith, James had confided to Thomas Davidson that he despaired of any popular religion of a philosophic character. Could any popular religion be raised "on the ruins of the old Christianity" without the presence of an element which had presided over the origin of all religions: a belief in new physical facts and possibilities? "Abstract considerations about the soul and the reality of a moral order will not do in a year," he protested, "what a glimpse into a world of new phenomenal possibilities enveloping those of the present life, afforded by an extension of our insights into the order of nature, would do in an instant." During the years that followed, James was often reproached by his professional colleagues—both scientists and philosophers—for an addiction to "intellectual bohemianism." They deplored his propensity to explore fields of experience cultivated only by "the scientific underworld." The frontier province of psychopathology, already discovered to be fertile in disturbing, repellent data, had not yet become officially, conventionally respectable. The phenomena produced by spiritualists, faith-healers and mental healers were in even worse case. Scientists ignored or despised them; the genteel public regarded them with indignant aversion. But it was largely by making excursions into these disreputable quarters that James extended his insight, for they furnished him with abundant evidence of new phenomenal possibilities.

Moreover, as James presently asserted, the border line between these dubious realms and that of true religious experience could not be accurately established. The institutions of religion, he insisted, were merely "secondary accretions upon a mass of concrete religious experiences." These experiences were connected with feelings and conduct which, as history proved, were perpetually renewed in the lives of humble private men. "If you ask what these experiences are," he declared, "they are conversations with the unseen, voices and visions, responses to prayer, changes of heart, deliverances from fear, inflowings of help, assurances of support, whenever certain persons set their own internal attitude in certain appropriate ways." These, for James, constituted the specific data of religion. Religion itself he defined in terms of "what goes on in the single private man." It is the feelings, acts and experiences of individual men in their solitude, so far as they apprehend themselves to stand in relation to whatever they may consider the divine.

It was from this standpoint that James dealt with religious experience in *The Varieties*, and he therefore described his book, in a subtitle, as a study in human nature. He regarded it "as in a sense a study of morbid psychology, mediating and interpreting to the philistine much that he would otherwise despise and reject utterly." For the book is not a descriptive analysis of secondhand religious life, that of the ordinary believer whose faith is predetermined by the prevailing religious traditions of his time and place. It sets forth the experiences of individuals for whom religion exists not as dull habit but as an acute fever; "geniuses in the religious line," as James termed them, men and women of exalted emotional sensibility, subject to abnormal psychical visitations and presenting innumerable peculiarities ordinarily classed as pathological. Yet the presumptively morbid origin of their religious life, as James emphasized, has no bearing upon its significance. To the contrary, he asserted, the coincidence in an individual of a superior intellect and a psychopathic temperament provides the best possible condition for "the kind of effective genius that gets into the biographical dictionaries." Such individuals do not remain mere intellectual critics or under-standers; their ideas obsess them, and they inflict their ideas, for better or worse, on their associates or their time. In short, if there is such a thing as inspiration from a higher realm, the neurotic temperament may well furnish the chief condition of a requisite receptivity to it.

To prove that such inspiration exists, James assembled and interpreted, in *The Varieties,* a massive anthology of human documents, firsthand accounts of those experiences which he enumerated as constituting the specific data of religious life. Declaring that nothing can be more stupid than to ignore phe-nomena merely because we ourselves are incapable of taking part in anything like them, he asserted that the religious beliefs to which these phenomena gave rise can be evaluated only by spiritual judgments directly passed upon them. Such judgments are based primarily on our own immediate feeling, and sec-ondarily on the experiential relevancy of the beliefs to our moral needs and to the rest of what we hold as true. As criteria of the spiritual significance both of experiences and of consequent beliefs, James proposed "immediate luminousness, philosophical reasonableness, and moral helpfulness." Essentially, these criteria are those imposed by the pragmatic method and theory of truth. They imply the direct evidence of fact, the consistency of such fact with previous truths, and the usefulness for future conduct of the new belief. Religious life, James held, is to be judged by its results; religious beliefs, by their vital fruits.

In the description of religious experience, James was not content to rely on the inherent plausibility of his documents. Since it was as much his purpose to justify religion as to study it, he spoke as the advocate of his witnesses; indeed, as their champion. Their extraordinary persuasiveness, as they follow one another in *The Varieties,* is often less due to their own testimony than to the eloquence and sympathy with which James interpreted it. His method was not that of the scientific analyst, but that of the creative artist. He entered into the consciousness of his witnesses, evoking the peculiar qualities of their suffering, or need, or aspiration, and reconstituting in all its original luminousness and cogency the particular experience that proved, in each instance, to be decisive for a spiritual biography. The range of James's capacity for empathy is impressively demonstrated by *The Varieties*. Here, for example, are to be found such dissimilar witnesses as George Fox, John Bunyan, Luther, Emerson and Tolstoi; Jacob Boehme, Saint Teresa, Saint John of the Cross, and many Oriental mystics; missionaries, revivalists, cardinals and priests; leaders of the New Thought movement; and a multitude of anonymous folk, representing all walks of life, whose personal accounts were made available to James. The immediate effect, as James intended, is to make the reader perceive the enormous diversities exhibited by the spiritual life of individuals. Submitting these diversities to "our ordinary worldly way of judging," he reminded his readers that the essence of religious experiences, by which they must finally be appraised, is that element or quality which they possess in common and uniquely, since it is to be found nowhere else.

This element or quality is the individual's overwhelming and inexpugnable awareness of communion—direct, active and mutual—with higher, unseen powers. Its reality is certified by immediate intuition, and it is therefore an absolute datum. James asserted that a single uniform process operates through the radical diversities of individual spiritual lives. He described it as the emergence of an uneasiness and the discovery of a solution. The uneasiness arises from a conviction that there is something wrong with us as we naturally stand, and the solution is the sense that we are saved from this wrongness by making proper connection with higher powers. The imputed wrongness has a moral character, and the salvation takes on a mystical tinge. When the state of salvation has been achieved, the individual identifies his real self with a higher self which has been revealed by the experience of being saved. He does so, James stated, by becoming conscious that this higher self is conterminous and continuous with a "more" of the same quality, operative in the universe outside him, with which he can thenceforth keep in working touch.

Regarding this process as fundamental to all religious experience, James attached special importance, in *The Varieties*, to the testimony of those whose spiritual lives displayed it most clearly: the sick souls, and the mystics. In their lives, the phenomena of acute despair, self-surrender, and a redemption, or second birth, are pronounced. Their testimony affirms that the individual must die to an unreal life before being saved by contact, or identification, with a supernatural consciousness. The whole weight of evidence from this quarter, as James acknowledged, demonstrates the inadequacy of the religion of healthy-mindedness, "because the evil facts which it refuses positively to account for are a genuine portion of reality; and they may after all be the best key to life's significance, and possibly the only openers of our eyes to the deepest levels of truth."

An indication of James's personal beliefs may be useful for the understanding of his final philosophy of religion. He acknowledged his inability to accept either popular Christianity or scholastic theism. His convictions ran counter to the rationalism and so-called liberalism which, in the first decade of the twentieth century, were the most characteristic tendencies of American Protestantism. James professed a supernaturalism of the "crasser" rather than the "more refined" type. By this he meant that he assigned the supernatural and the natural to the same level of reality. The supernaturalism that he professed, he said, "admits miracles and providential leadings, and finds no intellectual difficulty in mixing the ideal and the real worlds together by interpolating influences from the ideal region among the forces that causally determine the real world's details." For James, as he once remarked, the ideal, or supernatural, and the real, or natural, were dynamically continuous. However, he confessed that he had no living sense of commerce with a God; he envied those who had. But, although this was lacking to him, he asserted that "there is *something in me* which *makes response* when I hear utterances from that quarter made by others. I recognize the deeper voice. Something tells me: 'thither lies truth . . .' "

This intuition is central to James's philosophy of religion. It would have been oddly at variance with the reverence for fact affirmed by his radical empiricism had he not accounted it a fact which carried objective significance. The fundamental claim of all religious faiths is that "the conscious person is continuous with a wider self through which saving experiences come." James held this claim to be literally and objectively true. In part from his prolonged investigation of the phenomena of spiritualism, in part from his study of exceptional mental states, he had drawn one fixed conclusion which, he said, asserted itself dogmatically. He stated it as a theory: "There is a continuum of cosmic consciousness, against which our individuality builds but accidental fences, and into which our several minds plunge as into a mother-sea or reservoir." This other dimension of existence—which can be called either the mystical or the supernatural region—must be considered the source of most of our ideal impulses, because in finite experience we find them possessing us in a way for which we cannot articulately account. We belong to this dimension, James argued, in a more intimate sense than that in which we belong to the natural world, for we belong in the most intimate sense wherever our ideals belong. Yet the supernatural dimension is not merely ideal. It produces verifiable effects in the natural world of everyday life. When we commune with it, James declared, work is actually done on our finite personalities; we are regenerated, or born anew, or are lifted to a higher level of consciousness; and in the natural world, consequences in the way of conduct follow on this change. The reality of the supernatural world is established by the fact that it produces real effects.

It is verifiable fact that the supernatural world precipitates an actual inflow of energy when we put ourselves in the faith-state or prayer-state. How does the transforming flow of energy take place? James answered this question as a psychologist, basing his answer on Frederick W. H. Myers's theory of the subliminal self, and "the wonderful explorations by Binet, Janet,

Breuer, Freud, Mason, Prince, and others, of the subliminal consciousness of patients with hysteria." James regarded the discovery of an extramarginal field of consciousness as the most important advance made in psychology during his lifetime, because it had revealed an entirely unsuspected peculiarity in the constitution of human nature. In the phenomenon of "prayerful communion," he asserted, certain kinds of incursion from the subconscious region take part. He offered the hypothesis that the subconscious mind is the channel of communication between our finite personalities and a wider world of being than that of our normal consciousness, which is circumscribed for adaptation to our external earthly environment. By holding open the "subliminal door," James affirmed, we can experience union with something larger than ourselves and in that union find peace. Through this door, higher energies filter in to increase our vital potential. Through this door, "It would seem as though transmundane energies, God, if you will, produced immediate effects within the natural world to which the rest of our experience belongs."

For James the practical needs and experiences of religion were sufficiently met by the belief that beyond each individual, and in a fashion continuous with him, there exists a larger power that is friendly to him and his ideals. This belief he alluded to as his "mystical germ." It was, he said, a very common germ; it created the rank and file of believers. But James was not a mystic in the traditional sense of likewise being a monist. His religious doctrine has been well described by Ralph Barton Perry as "a radical departure: a pluralistic mysticism, and an experimental supernaturalism." The larger power friendly to the individual and his ideals postulated by James is not, on the facts, required to be either infinite or solitary. The power might conceivably be only a larger and more godlike self, of which the finite self would then be only a "mutilated expression"; and the universe might conceivably be a polytheism—a collection of such selves, of different degrees of inclusiveness, with no absolute unity in it realized at all. This was the notion that James suggested in

Human Immortality. As an hypothesis, it is consistent with the metaphysics of his radical empiricism, which assumes the world to have existed from its origin in pluralistic form, as an aggregate or collection of higher and lower things and principles in which unity is in process of evolution. The outlines of the superhuman consciousness, or larger power, James acknowledged, must remain very vague, and the number of "functionally distinct 'selves' which it comports and carries has to be left entirely problematic." Thus it may be conceived of either polytheistically or monotheistically. But James felt the imperative need to assume that "the superhuman consciousness, however vast it may be, has itself an external environment and consequently is finite." His philosophy of religion accepted "along with the superhuman consciousness, the notion that it is not all-embracing, the notion, in other words, that there is a God, but that he is finite, either in power, or in knowledge, or in both at once."

So, in the end, James reconciled his mysticism with his religion of healthy-mindedness and the metaphysics of his radical empiricism. In his philosophy of religion, personal immortality remains an over-belief, for which empirical verification is lacking; it is therefore subject to the criteria of legitimacy adduced in *The Will to Believe.* James himself regarded immortality as a secondary point. If our ideals are only cared for in "eternity," he declared, we might be willing to resign their care to other hands than ours. His finite God and pluralistic universe offer no absolute guarantee of all-inclusive security. The possibility always remains that this world may be partly saved and partly lost. "The ordinary moralistic state of mind," James asserted, "makes the salvation of the world conditional upon the success with which each unit does its part." But for practical life, he regarded the *chance* of salvation as enough. The existence of this chance makes the pragmatic difference between a life the keynote of which is resignation, and a life of which the keynote is hope.

Viewing God as the "intimate soul and reason of the universe," as "the indwelling divine rather than the external creator," James's philosophy of religion viewed "human life as part and parcel of that deep reality." For man, through the prayer-state or faith-state, can participate directly in God's consciousness and life. This possibility is the real import of James's mysticism, and it is likewise the verifiable fact upon which his philosophy of religion is founded. As a datum, or ultimate fact, the mystical state of communion with God and participation in His life should, philosophically, have been assimilated to that "pure experience" which James postulated as the primary stuff of being. But, leaving his metaphysics incomplete, he did not work out this problem. To him, it appeared certain that empirical methods would tend to connect men, in imagination, with a "more living divine reality" than that postulated by the creeds of his time. "Let empiricism once become associated with religion, as hitherto, through some strange misunderstanding, it has been associated with irreligion," he prophesied, "and I believe a new era of religion as well as of philosophy will be ready to begin."

CHAPTER SEVEN

ETHICS AND SOCIAL CRITICISM

"ALL God's life opens into the individual particular, and here and now, or nowhere, is reality." So William James declared in his address commemorating Emerson, and he quoted Emerson's great statement of this truth: "The present hour is the decisive hour, and every day is doomsday." No philosopher has felt more intensely than James the vivid dramatic quality of human existence. The individual's life, as it presented itself to him, is an affair of perpetual choices and rejections, any of which may have momentous consequences; and it is therefore a process in which ethics are deeply involved. James was intuitively an artist, and inherently a moralist. Oddly enough, he wrote nothing whatever for publication on the subject of art, and only a single essay on the subject of ethics.

James's total work, however, affirms a consistent moral attitude. This colors all his writing. Whatever his topic or subject, the habit of his mind compelled him to consider its ethical implications, and the light of his moral insight flashes out, on nearly every page, in an incidental reference or pungent example. It is here that his affinity with Emerson becomes most evident; but, more significantly, he shared certain of Emerson's convictions. During his later years, James's strong moral bent led him to take an active role in public affairs. The war with Spain and the issue of American imperialism aroused his conscience; he felt obliged to protest, and he vigorously tried to influence popular opinion. He gave his support to various projected reforms and other causes, speaking and writing in their behalf. This increasing participation in social and political controversy awakened him to 'the direction that American life was taking at the turn of the century. Until then, his optimism about the American future had been confident. In 1850 his father had declared that "our entire system of trade, as based upon what is called 'unlimited competition,' is a system of rapacity and robbery." But, during most of his career, William James paid little attention to the drastic changes that were transforming American society. He was scarcely aware of the social and economic context in which his philosophy had been developed, or of its implications within that context. In the last decade of his life, however—as his correspondence and much of his later writing abundantly reveal—he was absorbed, with a sense of sudden discovery, by the harsh new realities whose existence he had previously ignored. The effect of this belated enlightenment was to make him a sternly challenging critic of the American social order.

The source of James's moral philosophy is his reverence for, and faith in, the individual. His deepest and most obstinate convictions were those which he shared with Emerson. He believed profoundly in living at firsthand, in nonconformity. He asserted the indefeasible right to be precisely what one is, provided one only be authentic. "The present man is the aboriginal reality," he declared; "the Institution is derivative, and the past man is irrelevant and obliterate for present issues." He held, too, that "the highest good can be achieved only by our getting our proper life; and that can come about only by the help of a moral energy born of the faith that in some way or other we shall succeed in getting it if we try pertinaciously enough." These convictions accorded with his psychological doctrine that every consciousness is a fighter for ends, and they exemplified his gospel of the will to believe. The radical question of life—whether the universe is, at bottom, a moral or an unmoral one—cannot be solved until all the evidence is in, at the end of things. Meanwhile, we have to take our stand on one or the other assumption, and act as if it were true. The results of action will either corroborate or refute our hypothesis. As experience accumulates, they will tend to be increasingly consistent with it, or inconsistent. But, as James pointed out, inertia is the ultimate creed of the moral skeptic, energy that of the convinced moralist. Since the test of belief is action, doubt is practically equivalent to dogmatic negation, and "skepticism in moral matters is an active ally of immorality." Faith in a potentially moral universe is not only legitimate but practically efficacious. The world is what we make it, and we can make it good.

In his single essay on ethics, "The Moral Philosopher and the Moral Life," James argued that "there can be no final truth in ethics, any more than in physics, until the last man has had his experience and said his say." Insofar as we contribute to the race's moral life, we all help to determine the content of ethical philosophy. Our individual hypotheses, and the acts to which they prompt us, are positive contributions which actually change our environment. They create reality temporally, day by day; in so doing, they enrich or impoverish its moral, or ideal, values. Psychologically considered, many of our moral perceptions, or ideals, can only be explained as directly felt intuitions. They often contradict all the prepossessions of habit and presumptions of utility. "All the higher, more penetrating ideals are revolutionary," James declared. "They present themselves far less in the guise of effects of past experience than in that of probable causes of future experience, factors to which the environment and the lessons it has so far taught us must learn to bend." Moral judgments are the expression of subjective preferences or desires, and ideals are imperative only insofar as they are felt to be so. Any ideal, therefore, makes itself valid by the fact that it exists. Thus ethics have a genuine and real foothold in the finite world, and whether or not a God exists, we form an "ethical republic."

How, then, shall we define "the good"? The definition which James offered laid a groundwork for his later assertion, in *Pragmatism*, that "the right" is only the expedient in the way of our behaving. The essence of good, he declared, is simply to satisfy demand. The demand may be for anything under the sun. Goods are pluralistic, since value ultimately derives from the interests of the individual. In our everyday world the actually possible is vastly narrower than all that is demanded, and there is thus an incessant competition between conceived goods, or ideals. Furthermore, we are born into a society whose ideals are already largely ordered, and this still further limits the possibility that any of our individual ideals may be realized, particularly if they be revolutionary. In these circumstances, the guiding principle of ethics must be to satisfy as many demands as possible. "That act must be the best act, accordingly," James asserted, "which makes for the best whole, in the sense of awakening the least sum of dissatisfactions." Those ideals must be reckoned best which prevail at the least cost, and by whose realization the least possible number of other ideals are denied or destroyed. "Since victory and defeat there must be, the victory to be philosophically prayed for is that of the more inclusive side—of the side which even in the hour of triumph will to some degree do justice to the ideals in which the vanquished party's interests lay." Individualism is fundamental, but the maximum of social satisfaction is both the objective goal and the overruling principle of ethics. By following this principle, James held, "society has shaken itself into one sort of relative equilibrium after another by a series of social discoveries quite analogous to those of science."

This suggests that existing laws and usages are what yield the maximum collective satisfaction, and that ideals which accord with prevailing customs of the community are most entitled to support. But so universal a conformity, so static a morality, were fundamentally repugnant to James. He protested that there is nothing final in any actually given equilibrium of human ideals. Just as our present laws and customs have fought and conquered antecedent ones, so in turn they will be displaced by any newly discovered order which eliminates the complaints that they still give rise to, without producing others even more clamorous. Society is thus forever in flux, and every now and then an individual's revolutionary ideal or action may produce fruitful results.

An individual hazards much in breaking away from established rules and seeking to realize a larger ideal whole than they permit. But it is "at all times open to anyone to make the experiment, provided he fear not to stake his life and character on the throw." By breaking old moral rules at some point, the individual may inaugurate a total condition of things more ideal than would have obtained had the rules been maintained. By insisting upon absolute ethical distinctions and unconditional thou-shalt-nots, James asserted, social theorists of dogmatic temper change "a growing, elastic and continuous life into a superstitious system of relics and dead bones." In point of fact, he insisted, there are no absolute evils, and there are no nonmoral goods; and "the *highest* ethical life—however few may be called to bear its burdens—consists at all times in the breaking of rules which have grown too narrow for the actual case." A democratic society, therefore, will always have to decide, through actual experiment, by what kind of conduct the maximum amount of good can be gained and preserved. And its experiments cannot be judged by any absolute or a priori standards. They can be judged only by their results; by actually finding, after the experiments are made, "how much more outcry or how much appeasement comes about."

Social mutations, from generation to generation, James held, are on the whole due directly or indirectly to the acts, or the examples, of individuals who become ferments and initiators of movement, either because their genius is adapted to the receptivities of the moment, or because their accidental position of authority is critical. Social evolution, therefore, is the result of two wholly distinct factors: the individual, and the existing social environment. The individual derives his peculiar gifts from the play of physiological and infrasocial forces; but he brings to the social situation all the power of initiative and innovation. The social environment always exercises the power of accepting or rejecting the individual and his gifts. At any particular moment, a society offers ambiguous possibilities of development, and may respond to any of the alternative ideals then proposed. The accidental success of the new ideal will establish it, while its accidental failure will eliminate it. But the fluidity, or indeterminism, of society is not absolute. The accumulated social results of many past choices between alternatives are always operative in the immediate situation, and their effect is to exclude the possibility of the adoption of certain ideals. But the results of past choices do not positively define what further new ideals shall be accepted, for they have no power to fix the nature of the ideals which individuals may propose. It is the propitious interaction of individual and evironment that produces social change. Without the impulse or power of initiative of the individual, the community stagnates. Without the affirmative sympathy of the community, the impulse dies away. James forthrightly declared his adherence to the "great man" theory of history, which in the last quarter of the nineteenth century was being attacked by such evolutionary philosophers as Herbert Spencer and John Fiske. He denounced their doctrines as "the most pernicious and immoral of fatalisms." Talking only in terms of averages and general laws and predetermined tendencies, they ignored the immense importance of individual differences. The sphere of the race's average, no matter how large, James held, "is a dead and stagnant thing, an achieved possession, from which all insecurity has vanished"; and he asserted that the ultimate social fact is the power of initiative of the individual.

Affirming the primary social value of individual variations, James preached against "a certain blindness in human beings" that makes for intolerance of all deviations from the pattern which the established social order seeks to impose. We are all blind to the feelings of people different from ourselves, and our judgments concerning the significance of alien lives are warped by injustice and stupidity. The genuine significance of an individual's life lies in the particular feelings, aspirations and strivings that make him unique. They are authentic for him, but their authenticity is revealed to him alone. They are, however, the basis of social evolution, and if progress is to be made they must not be ignored or nullified. So James urged the cultivation of insight into individual differences, and an appreciation of their value. The practical consequence of this doctrine, he alleged, is an outward tolerance of whatever is not itself intolerant—"the well-known democratic respect for the sacredness of individuality."

Society itself, and all social institutions of whatever grade, James affirmed, are secondary and ministerial. They exist to serve man, not to standardize him; their function is instrumental. Believing that the individual is the fundamental phenomenon, James proclaimed his faith in personal freedom and its spontaneities. He viewed with suspicion "this intensely worldly social system of ours, in which each human interest is organized so collectively and commercially." He professed a decreasing respect for "civilization, with its herding and branding, licensing and degree-giving, authorizing and appointing, and in general regulating and administering by system the lives of human beings." Although society is perpetually in flux and continuously experimental, group interests favored by the existing situation will always try to make that situation permanent. To the degree that society sacrifices plasticity to organization, James held it to be stagnant and suspect. He urged Americans to remember that however many are the interests which a social system satisfies, there are always unsatisfied interests remaining over, and among them are interests "to which system, as such, does violence whenever it lays its hand upon us." The best commonwealth, and the best society, he affirmed, "will always be the one that most cherishes the men who represent the residual interests, the one that leaves the highest scope to their peculiarities." The very bone and marrow of life, he declared, is the obstinate insisting that tweedledum is *not* tweedledee.

In such warnings as this, James expressed his anxiety about the direction of social change in the United States. He welcomed the immense scientific and technological conquests of the industrial era. They proved that environment was malleable, and man essentially creative; they implied the promise of a better future. But as he became more and more familiar with their

immediate social consequences, James was disenchanted. He
disliked what he saw, and he was profoundly dubious about what
appeared predictable. The moralist in him, as well as the non-
conformist, protested against the new cult of bigness and greatness. The Spanish-American War provoked him to indignant
public repudiation of national policy committed to a selfish im-
perialistic adventure. But it was the aftermath of the war that,
quite literally, moved him to denounce the current aims and
objectives of his countrymen. Having driven the Spanish from
the Philippine Islands, the American Army was being used to
suppress and crush an insurrection, led by Aguinaldo, to achieve
national independence. James drew a scathing indictment of this
ruthless conquest which proclaimed a doctrine of racial su-
periority and was inspired by economic greed; a conquest which,
as he saw it, was destroying a people's freedom for the mere
financial advantage of business interests. It was, he alleged,
piracy positive and absolute: "On its face it reeked of the infernal
adroitness of the great department store, which has reached
perfect expertness in the art of killing silently and with no public
squealing or commotion the neighboring small concern." If this
exemplified modern civilization, civilization was no more than
a bloated idol, a "big, hollow, resounding, corrupting, sophisti-
cating, confusing torrent of mere brutal momentum and irra-
tionality." The infamy and iniquity of a war of conquest must
stop, James insisted. For the first time, he was ashamed of his
country, and he deplored the new American belief "in a national
destiny which must be 'big' at any cost, and which for some
inscrutable reason it has become infamous for us to disbelieve
in or refuse."

To a friend, James wrote in explanation of his position. He
was convinced that the bigger the unit you deal with, the hollower,
the more brutal, the more mendacious is the life displayed. He
was therefore against bigness and greatness in all their forms;
"against all big organizations as such, national ones first and
foremost; against all big successes and big results; and in favor
of the eternal forces of truth which always work in the individual

and immediately unsuccessful way, underdogs always, till history comes, after they are long dead, and puts them on the top." In the era of the great trusts, the developing monopolistic structures of finance capitalism, James looked at these results of "progress" and condemned them unreservedly. The new element of bigness in American civilization, he told H. G. Wells, had bred a national disease: "the exclusive worship of the bitch-goddess Success." On the word "success," Americans were putting only a squalid cash interpretation. This was producing a moral flabbiness, a callousness to abstract justice which James regarded as sinister, incomprehensible blots on the nation's life. "Every great institution is perforce a means of corruption—whatever good it may also do," he told another friend. "Only in the free personal relation is full ideality to be found."

Viewing American society at the turn of the century, James sometimes thought that the higher heroisms and the old rare flavors were passing out of life. Where now was the American who, like Louis Agassiz, would proudly announce that he had no time for making money? The "bosom-vices" of twentieth-century America impressed James as being merely mean and ignoble. He enumerated them publicly: "They are swindling and adroitness, and cant, and sympathy with cant—natural fruits of that extraordinary idealization of 'success' in the mere outward sense of 'getting there,' and getting there on as big a scale as we can, which characterizes our present generation." Even the universities, he felt, guaranteed little but a more educated cleverness in the service of popular idols and vulgar ends. He asserted that "our undisciplinables are our proudest product," and ranged himself among the enemies of the new religion of success. Eventually, he discovered great areas of heroism in the American social landscape. They were, he said, in the daily lives of the laboring classes.

Detesting the universal worship of the bitch-goddess Success, James declared that the prevalent fear of poverty among the educated classes is the worst moral disease from which our civilization suffers. "We despise anyone who elects to be poor in order to simplify and save his inner life. If he does not join the general scramble and pant with the moneymaking street, we deem him spiritless and lacking in ambition." The desire to gain wealth and the fear to lose it, James held, are our chief breeders of cowardice and propagators of corruption.

Think of the strength which personal indifference to poverty would give us if we were devoted to unpopular causes. We need no longer hold our tongues or fear to vote the revolutionary or reformatory ticket. Our stocks might fall, our hopes of promotion vanish, our salaries stop, our club doors close in our faces; yet, while we lived, we would imperturbably bear witness to the spirit, and our example would help to set free our generation.

It was as a breeder of false values that James most resented the new cult of power and wealth which, as he said, constitutes so large a portion of the "spirit" of our age.

He did not hesitate, therefore, to assert that democracy was on its trial, and that nobody could foretell how it would stand the ordeal. Was the irremediable destiny of Americans no more than vulgarity enthroned and institutionalized, elbowing everything superior from the highway? There were those who had already begun to draw Uncle Sam with the hog instead of the eagle for his emblem. Democracy as a whole, James acknowledged, may undergo self-poisoning. But on the other hand, among Americans democracy is a kind of religion, and they are bound not to admit its failure. The best Americans, James asserted, were still filled with the vision of "a democracy stumbling through every error till its institutions glow with justice and its customs shine with beauty." In the long run, James was willing to put his faith in the "civic genius" of the American people. This he defined as two inveterate habits carried into public life. "One of them is the habit of trained and disciplined good temper towards the opposite party when it fairly wins its innings. . . . The other is that of fierce and merciless resentment toward every man or set of men who break the public peace." These habits, in James's view, constituted the only bulwark of a democracy as yet neither secure nor fully vindicated. Should they ever fail, he prophesied, "neither laws nor monuments, neither battleships nor public libraries, nor great newspapers, nor booming stocks; neither mechanical invention nor political adroitness, nor churches nor universities nor civil service examinations can save us from degeneration . . ."

Yet notwithstanding his disenchantment and his doubts, James loved his country, as he said, for her youth, her greenness, her plasticity, innocence, good intentions. From Europe he wrote to a colleague that "we must thank God for America; and hold fast to every advantage of our position." He was an habitual, even a hereditary, traveller and sufficiently a cosmopolitan to feel, from time to time, that life in Europe was more congenial to him than life at home. But these moods were transient, and he was incapable of becoming, like his brother Henry, a permanent expatriate. He was convinced, as he told Charles Eliot Norton, that "a man coquetting with too many countries is as bad as a bigamist, and loses his soul altogether." He urged Norton not to despair of the United States:

> We've thrown away our old privileged and prerogative position among the nations, but it only showed that we were less sincere about it than we supposed we were. The eternal fight of liberalism has now to be fought by us on much the same terms as in the older countries. We have still the better chance in our freedom from all the corrupting influences from on top from which they suffer.

For, once in Europe, James was usually impressed by the seamy side of European life. The Dreyfus trial in France, with its repercussions everywhere on the Continent, increased his respect for his native land. America, he declared to another friend, knew no such corruption as Europe. In Europe the forces of corruption were rooted and permanent, while in the United States the only permanent incentive was party spirit. Millionaires and syndicates had their immediate cash to pay, James acknowledged, but they had no intrenched prestige to work with like, in Europe, the church sentiment, the army sentiment, the aristocracy and royalty sentiment, which could be brought to bear in favor of every kind of individual and collective crime—appealing not only to the immediate pocket of the persons to be corrupted but to the ideals of their imagination likewise.

James defined his attitude to political and social issues as that of a liberal, and he surmised that liberals were destined to be a permanent minority. "Often their only audience is posterity. Their names are first honored when the breath has left their bodies, and, like the holders of insurance policies, they must die to win their wager . . ." He believed the strongest force in politics to be human scheming, and acknowledged that the schemers, or professional politicians, would inevitably capture every machinery that could be set up against them. The chronic fault of liberalism, he admitted, is its lack of speed and passion. He particularly deplored the influence, on American public opinion, of the sensational popular press: "Now illiteracy has an enormous literary organization, and power is sophistical; and the result is necessarily a new phenomenon in history—involving every kind of diseased sensationalism and insincerity in the collective mind." To offset the power of the professional politicians and the cheap press, James proposed that American liberals—the "intellectuals," he called them, after the defenders of Dreyfus in France—develop their own "class-consciousness" and organize politically. In the conflicting currents of American life they might exercise only a relatively insignificant energy, yet "a small force, if it never lets up, will accumulate effects more considerable than those of much greater forces if these work inconsistently." Too many American intellectuals, James charged, nursed the notion that ideals are self-sufficient and require no actualization. This was not "healthy-minded"; it was "a kind of resignation and sour grapes." Ideals, James insisted, ought to aim at the transformation of reality—no less. Was it not, therefore, the moral obligation of American intellectuals to work actively to preserve the precious national birthright of individualism and freedom? "The ceaseless whisper of the more permanent ideals, the steady tug of truth and justice, give them but time," he asserted, "*must* warp the world in their direction."

At the end of his life, James looked forward hopefully to this process of "changing prevalent ideals." He wrote to his brother Henry: "Stroke upon stroke, from pens of genius, the competitive regime so idolized seventy-five years ago, seems to be getting wounded to death. What will follow will be something better . . ." In the very last essay which he wrote, he declared: "I devoutly believe in the reign of peace, and in the gradual advent of some sort of a socialistic equilibrium." This essay, widely reprinted, was "The Moral Equivalent of War," in which James reinforced his argument against militarism by a project for sublimating the martial spirit and harnessing it to the collective social welfare. His project—long afterward to be approximated by the Civilian Conservation Corps of President Franklin Roosevelt's administration—was a universal conscription of youth "to form for a certain number of years a part of the army enlisted against *Nature*." But more remarkable than this suggestion was James's candid avowal of widespread social injustice in the United States, and his indignation that "so many men, by mere accidents of birth and opportunity, should have a life of *nothing else* but toil and pain and hardness and inferiority imposed upon them . . ." Some form of renovation of the existing social system, he implied, was necessary. "All the qualities of a man acquire dignity when he knows that the service of the collectivity that owns him needs them. If proud of the collectivity, his own pride rises in proportion." The collectivity represented by an industrialized, commercialized, materialistic America aroused no pride in James; it evoked only the emotion of shame. His plea, therefore, was for a "superior collectivity," and this he thought he discerned in "the more or less socialistic future towards which mankind seems drifting."

Yet, in ways of which James himself seemed to be scarcely aware, his philosophy could be invoked to justify precisely those tendencies in American life whose consequences he most deplored. Its insistence on individualism, its emphasis on action and practical results, its criterion of success, its doctrine of expediency, its inherent relativism—all these elements were susceptible of misinterpretation. In a competitive and acquisitive society that exalted the goals of wealth and power, the notion that whatever "works" is right could be perverted to sanction nearly all forms of economic or social abuse. James's denial of the authority of ethical absolutes furnished a convenient support for moral cynicism. His assertion that the essence of good is simply to satisfy demand provided a creed for materialism. As measures of value, his criteria of instrumental expediency and efficacy appeared to authorize the very practices which, in his later role of social critic, he so forthrightly denounced. During the prolonged controversy over pragmatism, James frequently sought to dispel the "preposterous misunderstanding" with which he felt the doctrine had been received. He denied that pragmatism is "a sort of bobtailed scheme of thought, excellently fitted for the man on the street, who naturally hates theory and wants cash returns immediately." That pragmatists had laid more stress on human action than any previous philosophers, he acknowledged; but he insisted that "pragmatism's primary interest is in its doctrine of truth." "Instead of being a practical substitute for philosophy, good for engineers, doctors, sewage experts, and vigorous untaught minds in general to feed upon," he declared, "pragmatism has proved so over-subtle that even academic critics have failed to catch its question, to say nothing of their misunderstanding of its answer." But James never attempted to defend his philosophy from misapplication in the spheres of economic activity and social policy. His knowledge of economics was, at best, superficial, and for most of his life he was ignorant of the new economic forces that were transforming the American social order, and thus exercising a decisive influence on the lives and destinies of his fellow-citizens. That his doctrines could be appealed to for the defense of a "corporate collectivism" so far as possible exempt from social accountability was a contingency that James did not envisage. Had he foreseen it, he might have reinforced his social criticism with a social theory. But in this respect his philosophy remained incomplete, and it was John Dewey who, after James's death, systematically developed the economic and social implications of pragmatism.

CHAPTER EIGHT

THE INFLUENCE OF WILLIAM JAMES

IN 1903 John Dewey described the *Principles* as the "spiritual progenitor" of the insurgent movement in philosophy which, under his leadership, had been launched at the University of Chicago. Later that year, he wrote to James and alluded to "all the points in which your psychology 'already' furnishes the instrumentalities for a pragmatic logic, ethics and metaphysics . . ." The influence of William James on American speculative thought is most notably exemplified by Dewey's massive, varied philosophical works.

By the middle of the twentieth century, James's major doctrines had directly affected the lives of two generations of Americans, many of whom may never have heard his name. This, also, was due to John Dewey, whose radical innovations in educational theory had pervaded almost every classroom in the United States. Probably never before in history had a philosophy been applied so hopefully, or so nearly universally, to discipline the minds of youth, from earliest childhood, to the uses of a greater freedom. In effect, the far-reaching reform of education inspired by Dewey carried into social practice both the fundamental theories of James's functional psychology and the central theses of his philosophy. That the knower is an actor; that ideas, being plans for action, can produce changes in the external world and so create their truth: these contentions, first advanced by James during the 1870's, eventually transformed the American school.

Both politics and sociology have been influenced by the thought of William James. The program of the Progressive revolt of 1912, under the leadership of Theodore Roosevelt, applied pragmatic ideas to political issues. When Woodrow Wilson, as President, declared that the word "progress" was almost a new one, and that the modern idea was to leave the past and press on to something new, he was speaking as James's disciple. In demanding from Congress the notable "reform" measures enacted during his first administration, Wilson repeatedly asserted the pragmatic doctrine that existing political and social institutions must be adapted to changing conditions. But the most significant political application of James's ideas was made by President Franklin D. Roosevelt. Pragmatism supplied the philosophy and thus helped shape the program of the New Deal. The New Deal assumed society to be plastic, and environment to be amenable to change. It adopted the theory of social experiment, and it justified experiments by their expediency and their results. It held that social, political and economic institutions are primarily instruments, and that their essential function is to promote the general welfare; that they are subject to deliberate control and may be altered when found defective.

These principles, first carried into government during the 1930's, had long been regarded as axioms in the narrower sphere of applied sociology. Social theorists like Jane Addams and Lillian D. Wald had made them the foundation of complex organizations which, developing from experimental methods of meeting problems as they arose, established techniques for dealing with social maladjustment and inaugurated services that later became public functions. In general, James's vision of a society forever in flux, and an environment perpetually susceptible of transformation in accord with human needs and desires, has come to dominate the philosophy of reform.

The pragmatic way of thinking has also substantially affected jurisprudence. In his great, classic book *The Common Law,* Justice Oliver Wendell Holmes held that certainty is generally an illusion, and he discarded the historic concept of a "natural law" embodying eternal principles, forming an ultimate, immutable sanction. The law, like other mortal contrivances, Holmes asserted, is subject to chance and change. It has its roots in history and its justification in expediency, real or supposed. Its substance, at any given time, tends to correspond with what is then understood to be convenient; but its form and machinery, and the degree to which it is able to work out desired results, depend very much upon its past. The law, Holmes argued, is always approaching, but never reaching, consistency. It is forever adopting new principles from life, while retaining old ones from history which have become merely vestigial. Holmes therefore denied the binding force of judicial precedent, or tradition, upon the present, affirming that the present has a right to govern itself so far as it can. In a revolutionary statement, he declared that the life of the law has not been logic; it has been experience. This pragmatic doctrine led Holmes to formulate another radical conclusion. At any specific moment in history, he asserted, the basic rules of law are determined by the felt necessities of the time, the prevalent moral and political theories, institutions of public policy, avowed or unconscious, and even the prejudices which judges share with their fellow-men. The true source of the law, he claimed, is always to be found in considerations of what is expedient for the community concerned.

All of Justice Holmes's most celebrated opinions reflected his pragmatic philosophy of law. During his long service on the Supreme Court, he consistently interpreted the Constitution as a flexible charter for a society conceived as being itself dynamic, and proceeding by the method of trial and error. He vigorously defended the right of the American people to make "social experiments that an important part of the community desires, in the insulated chambers afforded by the several States, even though the experiments may seem futile or even noxious . . ." In one of his most widely quoted opinions, evoked by a case involving civil liberties, Holmes, directly paraphrasing William James, declared that "the best test of truth is the power of the thought to get itself accepted in the competition of the market." This, he affirmed, "is the theory of our Constitution. It is an experiment, as all life is an experiment. Every year if not every day we have to wager our salvation upon some prophecy based upon imperfect knowledge. While that experiment is part of our system I think that we should be eternally vigilant against attempts to check the expression of opinions that we loathe and believe to be fraught with death, unless they so imminently threaten immediate interference with the lawful and pressing purposes of the law that an immediate check is required to save the country."

Holmes's younger associate, Justice Louis D. Brandeis, likewise applied the doctrines of pragmatism both to social and economic theory, and to constitutional law. Before his appointment to the Supreme Court, and during his voluntary service as "counsel for the people," Brandeis—believing, like William James, in the primacy of the individual—frequently warned against "the curse of bigness" in the American economy. As a reformer, he chose to expound social principle in terms of hard economic facts. He put forward two ideas which had important results in the life of the nation. One was the doctrine of "social invention." The other was the theory of the "living law." Both were applications of pragmatism. By social invention, which he asserted was the most insistent need of the times, Brandeis meant the use, under democratic safeguards, of the experimental method in solving problems that generate social unrest. His own public legal work furnished a number of arresting illustrations which brought the doctrine nation-wide celebrity. But, to achieve genuine efficacy, social invention requires a foundation of legal validity. To provide this, Brandeis advanced his theory of a living law, which he expounded in several history-making cases that he argued before the Supreme Court, and which he afterwards emphasized in the opinions that he delivered as one of its members. Because the theory introduced a new concept into constitutional law, legal authorities consider it Brandeis's most conspicuous achievement. It represented an attempt to make the law responsive to what Holmes had described as "the felt necessities of the time."

Brandeis asserted that American law had not kept pace with the changes occurring in the fundamental conditions of American life. The longing of the American people had shifted from legal justice to social justice; the law had lagged behind. In the divorce of law from life, appeal was made to constitutional provisions to stop the natural vent of remedial legislation. Statutes based on new social facts were vetoed by the Supreme Court, which declared such facts immaterial and based its decisions not on life but on logic and precedent. Brandeis contended that industrialization of the American economy had invalidated many historic precedents; they were no longer applicable to existing conditions. Although the social sciences took account of the changes produced by industrialization, legal science—judge-made law, as distinguished from legislation—was largely deaf and blind. If the law was to be made responsive to the new needs developed by a changing social order, argument and judicial conclusions must be based not upon ancient abstractions but upon contemporary facts. They must be shifted from the barren ground of precedent and logic to the higher ground of social function and social situation. Brandeis held that the actual economic and social setting from which legislation emerges must be made the controlling factor in judicial decision as to its validity. Through his theory of a "living law," Brandeis established as elements of jurisprudence both the pragmatic method and the pragmatic theory of truth.

The great significance of James's *Principles* in the development of modern psychology and its pervasive general influence have already been noted. One of James's major contributions to psychology—his account of the process of thought and definition of the nature of consciousness—has deeply affected the literature of our time. James emphasized the continuous fluency of mental life. He named the "stream of consciousness." He ascribed a peculiar importance to its transitive portions, which exist as a penumbral fringe; a fringe that he later termed "the twilight region that surrounds the clearly lighted center of experience." William James's theory of the subjective flux had no discernible effect on the novels of his brother Henry, the greatest master of psychological fiction then writing in the English language. Henry James took a very different view of the nature of consciousness and spoke disparagingly of the possible use, in fiction, of "the terrible *fluidity* of self-revelation." His principal disciples, among them Joseph Conrad, heeded Henry James's warning and in general did not depart from his technical practice. But shortly after the first World War, William James's account of the stream of consciousness yielded radical innovations in the content and the technique of fiction. Such novelists as Dorothy Richardson and Virginia Woolf, by exploiting the "interior monologue," began to present directly the full mental life of characters, both in the clearly lighted center of experience and in the twilight region that surrounds it. Character, in fiction, thus acquired an additional dimension. And novelists were able, for the first time, to explore and actually represent the process of life described by William James in his statement that "experience is remoulding us every moment, and our mental reaction on any given thing is really a resultant of our experience of the whole world up to that date." Almost simultaneously, the theories of Sigmund Freud and Carl Jung expanded the range of the subjective flux, and there began to well up, in contemporary fiction, a darkly subconscious life; most notably, in James Joyce's *Ulysses*. But although the subsequent development of the psychological novel has been marked by increasing reliance on psychoanalysis, it is to James that contemporary writers owe their fundamental concept of consciousness, their ability to enlarge the dimensions of character, and their most fruitful technical device for the direct communication of experience.

The most important influence that William James has exercised is, perhaps, incalculable. Many of his ideas and much of his philosophy have entered the stream of popular American thought, and today form part of the intellectual equipment of the average citizen. James himself recognized the natural tendency of "satisfying" ideas to "filter in"; and on one occasion he confessed that his personal hopes were fixed on "the newer generation." He might have been dismayed, however, by the use to which they put some of his teaching. The career of the doctrine which he set forth in his essay on "The Energies of Men" serves as an eloquent illustration. In this essay James suggested that the subliminal consciousness is a storehouse of untapped powers available to the individual, and he cited certain disciplines as working efficaciously in releasing them. Did not this give scientific validity to the common American belief that anything may be accomplished by anybody, especially through the mastery of some esoteric technique? In the forty years after his death, the authority of William James was often invoked to promote various techniques of materialistic mysticism which, if cultivated perseveringly, would enable their disciples to establish high sales records, radiate "charm," acquire wealth, become outstanding, command wide influence, or enjoy a gratifying love life. There was an aspect of James's teaching which made this perversion of it almost inevitable. His doctrine of the "will to believe"—a phrase which he soon lamented as unfortunate—lent itself to grotesque misrepresentation. It has frequently been expounded as the counsel that faith in success is sufficient to bring success about; that blind assurance will be warranted by its results. However heartening to the muddle-headed, so dubious an evangel would have been repugnant to James. He did not identify the presumption of power and the possession of it.

The influence of James's religious doctrine has been more salutary and even more widespread. That the conscious person is continuous with a wider self through which saving experiences come, James declared a true hypothesis; true because it "worked." To many Americans, his pluralistic mysticism and experimental supernaturalism have provided a moral equivalent for the dogmas of theism which no longer compel their faith. Like James, they have had a "mystical germ." This germ has always been endemic in America. From the time of Jonathan Edwards to the present there have never been lacking in America spiritual leaders of a strongly mystical cast. Surprisingly enough, their attraction has often been most powerful when the nation's energies were absorbed by practical affairs. In the days of westward expansion, Emerson carried to the pioneers his gospel that the spiritual principle should be suffered to demonstrate itself to the end. During the era of industrialization, Mrs. Eddy gained her converts to Christian Science in the East, the Middle West and the Far West. The facts suggest that whenever materialistic incentives dominate the American people, an element of the native conscience is impelled to rebel against them, or repudiate them. Margaret Fuller once remarked that, in these circumstances, Americans often suffered a revulsion of sheer disgust and had "to quarrel with all that is, because it is not spiritual enough."

It was therefore not unnatural for William James's philosophy of religion to emerge from the swelling prosperity of the early twentieth century. To the American people, neither his mysticism nor his practical justification of it seemed especially novel. These merely provided a philosophical sanction for dormant, inarticulate, popular convictions. But James broke new ground in making religious mysticism scientifically respectable. This enabled the spiritually adrift to yield to their intuitions without violating their intelligence; it reconciled the religious impulse to the modern scientific spirit. As a result, the influence of James's religious doctrine has ultimately reached many Americans who possibly are unfamiliar with his books. In the churches, where religion was increasingly becoming identified with social good works, the effect of James's doctrine has been to restore a sense of the identity of man with God, and to define religion once again in exclusively spiritual terms. Upon theologians, James's influence is less easy to trace. Certainly he has provided a philosophical foundation for that contemporary defense of faith which discards the weapon of reason. The doctrine that faith is essentially nonrational, that it is a reality which reason can neither discover nor destroy and which science cannot imperil, has one of its sources in James's philosophy of religion. His concept of a God finite in power or knowledge, or both, has been adopted and elaborated in the *Philosophy of Religion* of Edgar Sheffield Brightman, who has used it, as James also did, in the philosophical solution of the problem of evil. And perhaps James's mysticism—as he might have been surprised to learn—has fertilized many of the esoteric cults which, after his death, sprang up and flourished under the sunny skies of California.

To the degree that they have entered the intellectual equipment of the average American, James's ideas and philosophy have strongly reinforced traditional convictions. During the second quarter of the twentieth century, the concept of determinism—economic, political and social—gained in authority, both in Europe and the United States. Many Americans continued to find it repugnant, and resisted it vigorously. The influence of James contributed to their confidence that the future could be made different and far better than the past, their faith in the creative function and resources of the individual, their emphasis on action as the outcome of thought. James taught that a man must take his part, believing something, acting in behalf of his belief, incurring the risk of being wrong. Many of his countrymen still considered this the best basis on which to conduct their lives, individually and collectively. "Believe that life *is* worth living," James said, "and your belief will help create the fact." At the middle of the century, Americans, on the whole, still lived in the light of that counsel.

Everything in the end, James declared, depended not upon mechanism, but on man, and especially upon the exercise of his moral will. Man's "practical control of nature," he pointed out, "accelerates so that no one can trace the limit; one may even fear that the *being* of man may be crushed by his own powers, that his fixed nature as an organism may not prove adequate to stand the strain of the ever increasingly tremendous functions, almost divine creative functions, which his intellect will more and more enable him to wield. He may drown in his wealth like a child in a bath-tub, who has turned on the water and who cannot turn it off." Nearly a half-century after James wrote it, this picture of man's possible destiny seemed tragically prophetic. Yet more than ever the vital questions seemed to be those which James had propounded at the same time. "Will you join the procession? Will you trust yourself and trust the other agents enough to face the risk?"

CHRONOLOGY

1842	Born Astor House, New York City (January 11)
1843–44	James family in Europe
1852–55	School in New York
1855–58	School and tutors in England and France
1859–60	School and tutors in Switzerland and Germany
1860–61	Studies painting with William Morris Hunt, Newport
1861	Enters Lawrence Scientific School, Harvard
1864	Enters Harvard Medical School
1865–66	On expedition to Brazil with Louis Agassiz
1867–68	In Germany for health and study
1869–72	Period of ill-health and recovery
1873	Appointed Instructor in Anatomy and Physiology at Harvard
1876	Appointed Assistant Professor of Physiology
1878	Marriage to Alice Howe Gibbens; undertakes treatise on Psychology
1879	Begins teaching philosophy
1880	Appointed Assistant Professor of Philosophy
1885	Appointed Professor of Philosophy
1898	Suffers injury to heart
1901–02	Delivers Gifford Lectures at Edinburgh
1906	Acting Professor at Stanford

1906–07 Lectures on Pragmatism, Lowell Institute and Columbia
1907 Retires from professorship at Harvard
1908–09 Delivers Hibbert Lectures at Oxford
1910 In Europe for health
1910 Dies at summer home, Chocorua, New Hampshire, August 26

BIBLIOGRAPHY
WORKS BY WILLIAM JAMES

The Literary Remains of the Late Henry James, edited by William James, New York, 1890.

Principles of Psychology, New York, Henry Holt, 1890.

Psychology, Briefer Course, New York, Henry Holt, 1892.

The Will to Believe, and Other Essays in Popular Philosophy, New York, Longmans, Green & Company, 1897.

Human Immortality: Two Supposed Objections to the Doctrine, Boston, Houghton Mifflin, 1898.

Talks to Teachers on Psychology: and to Students on Some of Life's Ideals, New York, Henry Holt, 1899.

The Varieties of Religious Experience: A Study in Human Nature, New York, Longmans, Green & Company, 1902.

Pragmatism: A New Name for Some Old Ways of Thinking, New York, Longmans, Green & Company, 1907.

The Meaning of Truth: A Sequel to "Pragmatism," New York, Longmans, Green & Company, 1909.

A Pluralistic Universe: Hibbert Lectures on the Present Situation in Philosophy, New York, Longmans, Green & Company, 1909.

*Some Problems of Philosophy: A Beginning of an Introduction to Philosophy,** New York, Longmans, Green & Company, 1911.

*Memories and Studies,** New York, Longmans, Green & Company, 1911.

*Essays in Radical Empiricism,** New York, Longmans, Green & Company, 1912.

*Collected Essays and Reviews,** New York, Longmans, Green & Company, 1920.

IMPORTANT WORKS RELATING TO WILLIAM JAMES

James, Henry, *A Small Boy and Others*, New York, Charles Scribner's Sons, 1913.

James, Henry, *Notes of a Son and Brother*, New York, Charles Scribner's Sons, 1914.

The Letters of William James; edited by his son Henry James (2 vols.), Boston, Little, Brown & Company, 1920.

Matthiessen, F. O., *The James Family, Including Selections from the Writings of Henry James, Senior, William, Henry, & Alice James*, New York, Alfred A. Knopf, 1947.

Perry, Ralph Barton, *Annotated Bibliography of the Writings of William James*, New York, Longmans, Green & Company, 1920.

Perry, Ralph Barton, *The Thought and Character of William James* (2 vols.), Boston, Little, Brown & Company, 1935.

* Posthumously published.

SELECTIVE INDEX